SLIDE

MOUNTAIN

SLIDE

MOUNTAIN

OR THE FOLLY OF

OWNING NATURE

Theodore Steinberg

University of California Press

BERKELEY LOS ANGELES

LONDON

University of California Press
Berkeley and Los Angeles, California

University of California Press
London, England

Copyright © 1995 by Theodore Steinberg

First Paperback Printing 1996

Library of Congress Cataloging-in-Publication Data
Steinberg, Theodore, 1961–
  Slide Mountain, or, The folly of owning nature / Theodore
Steinberg.
    p. cm.
  Includes bibliographical references and index.
  ISBN 0-520-20709-2 (alk. paper)
    1. Land tenure. 2. Land tenure—United States. 3. Land
use. 4. Land use—United States. 5. Real property. 6. Real
property—United States. I. Title. II. Title: Slide Mountain.
III. Title: Folly of owning nature.
HD1251.S74 1995
333.3'0973—dc20   94-25476
                                                        CIP

Printed in the United States of America

1 2 3 4 5 6 7 8 9

The paper used in this publication meets the minimum
requirements of American National Standard for Information
Sciences—Permanence of Paper for Printed Library Materials.
ANSI Z39.48-1984 ⊗

A portion of this book originally appeared in the Michigan Quarterly Review.

This work is supported, in part, by the New Jersey Institute
of Technology under Grant No. 421490.

Maps by Charlotte Zanecchia.

Photograph on p. 89 courtesy of Jack Birns, Life magazine © Time Warner;
photograph on p. 108 courtesy of Eric Schall, Life magazine © Time Warner; photograph
on pp. 142–143 courtesy of the Eno Collection, Miriam & Ira D. Wallach Division of Art,
Prints & Photographs, The New York Public Library, Astor, Lenox and Tilden
Foundations; photographs on pp. 158 and 169 are by the author.

For Maria

CONTENTS

ACKNOWLEDGMENTS

Deepest thanks are due the following people: Robert Cohen, David Morris, and Jim O'Brien, because their feel for language made this a better book and me a better writer; Dror Wahrman, because he helped me discover God and the moon; Michael Black, because of his sense of humor; Robert Hannigan, Bruce Mizrach, and Zoë Strother, because they pushed me to think a bit more carefully about what I was saying; David Fischer, Morton Horwitz, and Donald Worster, because for years they have stood behind me and my various ideas and escapades; and Sheila Berg, Michael Clark, Maria Del Monaco, Laurence Goldstein, Andrea Henderson, Stanley Holwitz, David Hsiung, James Hynes, Melissa Johnson, Michelle Johnson, Paul Karon, Larry Kramer, Arthur McEvoy, Daniel McShea, William Miller, Martin Reuss, A. W. Brian Simpson, Richard Tucker, James Boyd White, and Charlotte Zanecchia.

Nor could this book have been written without the financial support of the following institutions: the American Council of Learned Societies, the Horace H. Rackham School of Graduate Studies and the Michigan Society of Fellows at the University of Michigan, Ann Arbor, and the New Jersey Institute of Technology.

SLIDE

MOUNTAIN

Fast Fish in America:
An Introduction

*The first person who, having fenced off a plot of ground, took it into
his head to say* this is mine *and found people simple enough to
believe him, was the true founder of civil society.*
—J. J. ROUSSEAU (1755)

The most famous legal dispute in Nevada's history never
happened. It is a story that has been told many times, but
no one tells it better than Mark Twain. We begin about ten
miles north of Carson City in the Washoe Valley, hemmed
in on the west by mountains thousands of feet high. There
we find Slide Mountain, an uncertain terrain if ever there
was one.

One day back in the nineteenth century a group of prac-
tical jokers in Carson City set out to dupe a U.S. attorney
by the name of Buncombe. Dick Hyde, who was in on the
joke, came busting into Buncombe's office. A landslide, he
cried, had caused his neighbor Tom Morgan's ranch to slip
down on top of his property, burying it to a depth of thirty-
eight feet. Worse yet, Morgan now claimed possession of
both layers of real estate. Weeping, Hyde pleaded with Buncombe to represent his interests in the buried land. Buncombe agreed.

Justice was speedily attended to later that afternoon. The
judge, who was also in on the gag, listened to testimony and

then pretended to make up his mind: "Gentlemen, it ill becomes us, worms as we are, to meddle with the decrees of Heaven." If Heaven, he continued, chose to move the Morgan ranch to the benefit of its owner, then what right did mere mortals have to question the act's legality? "No— Heaven created the ranches and it is Heaven's prerogative to rearrange them." An act of God had deprived Hyde of his property, he ruled, and there was no appealing God's decision. Buncombe, incensed by the stupidity of the ruling, begged his honor to reconsider. After appearing to mull over the matter again, the judge told Buncombe that Hyde still had title to his land, a perfectly good right, that is, *to dig* his buried ranch out from under all thirty-eight feet of Morgan's property. Enraged by this gross miscarriage of justice, the U.S. attorney marched off in a huff. Buncombe, to put it mildly, had been had.[1]

But the joke, I'm afraid, was not on Buncombe alone. It is on us, all of us who consider ourselves property owners or who are forced to respect a world increasingly defined by private property rights. Twain is poking fun at a culture that had fallen in love with property. We (along with the jokers) chuckle at Buncombe's gullibility in the face of a tall tale, at his failure to see that the judge was drawing him on. But the more one reflects, the more apparent it is that Buncombe and the judge simply stretch our usual assumptions about property slightly beyond their normal limits. Imagine for a moment that Hyde *had* managed to dig out his buried ranch to gain possession of it once again, maybe secretly piling it atop Morgan's land. Would he own it? Perhaps. As the saying goes, possession *is* nine-tenths of the law—an assumption shared by Buncombe *and* the jokers, not to mention Twain's American audience. Buncombe fell for the ruse at least partly because the issues are more believable than one might think. Twain, however, is also playing a huge joke on our commonsense assumptions about property in land. Pushed to its limits, our property-centered view of the world contains the seeds of its own undoing.

The moral of the story is that real estate is not as real, solid, or lasting as it may seem. In other words, Dick Hyde lost something that he not only was not supposed to lose but that supposedly was not losable. Real property like land is supposed to stay put; that is what distinguishes it from, say, personal property, which can be moved or carried around. But as Twain shows, nature's complexity can at times make ownership a precarious, even unreal affair. In a sense, we all live in the shadow of Slide Mountain.

This book looks at the struggles of ordinary and not so ordinary people as they battled to own the natural world. It is set in the twentieth century, a century with an affinity for dominating nature that extends far beyond the comparatively mild appetite of Twain's frontier settlers. My task is to investigate a variety of changing modern environments— Slide Mountains all of them—and the dilemmas raised when they confronted the sometimes absurd provisions of modern property law.

Back in Twain's day, the ability to control nature was somewhat more tentative than in the century that followed. The judge in Twain's mock trial, for example, declared it best not to meddle in the affairs of nature, which were ultimately God's doings, and there were surely others—many, no doubt—who shared this theocentric view. By contrast, twentieth-century Americans have been far more secular and meddlesome. The monuments are everywhere to see: dams hundreds of feet high plugging the country's longest and most powerful rivers; sprawling cityscapes so choked with concrete and steel that nature is all but annihilated;

artificial wetlands to replace the ones that we have wrecked; irrigation wells dug so deep and pumped so hard that the surrounding land has all but collapsed. And then there are the monuments yet to materialize. These include a plan, first dreamed up by a Los Angeles engineer in the 1950s, to harness western Canada's abundant water and send it south to hydrate the arid American West. This modest proposal calls for reversing the flow of some of North America's largest rivers, for putting hundreds of thousands of Canadians off their land and turning that land into reservoirs, a plan so positively monstrous that it would cause Prince George, British Columbia—the entire city—to perish from the earth.[2] Twentieth-century America is a society obsessed with mastering nature technologically, a society bent on redesigning the natural world, no matter what the cost.

Much like science and technology, property law is yet another tool for imposing order on the chaos of nature. Most people recognize how thoroughly our modern technologies control the natural world—like a dam sending water off in ten different directions. But what does something as abstract as property law have to do with the control of nature? An example will help to explain.

Consider one of the oldest questions about property: How is it that some things get to be owned? The classic legal case on this issue, which no one escapes law school without learning, dates from 1805. On a May afternoon in that year, Lodowick Post and his dog did "upon a certain wild and uninhabited, unpossessed and waste land, called the beach, find and start one of those noxious beasts called a fox." It was not a good day for Post. Just as he rushed in for the kill, an interloper named Jesse Pierson shot the fox, swung it over his shoulder, and headed off. In the legal case that ensued before a New York court, the matter turned on one simple question: Who owned the fox? In Judge Tompkins's view, Pierson did. He reasoned as follows. Chasing the fox was one thing, but to establish a property right it was necessary to mortally wound the animal, thereby bringing the creature within "certain control" and confirming possession, on which ownership rests.[3]

Pierson v. *Post* demonstrates an essential fact about the common law of property: it is predicated on the "control" of nature (in this case, a wild animal, but it could be any element of the nonhuman world). Control over the fox established Pierson's property right. Put simply, control confers possession, and possession is at the root of title.

The question then is, What is meant by possession? An answer, or at least the beginning of one, was offered by Carol Rose in a 1985 article that appeared in the *University of Chicago Law Review*. In her view, possession amounts to a statement of ownership. By killing the fox, Pierson put the world on notice about his intention to appropriate the animal. Possession, in Rose's opinion, is an act of communication. As she puts it, "The first to say, 'This is mine,' in a way that the public understands, gets the prize, and the law will help him keep it against someone else who says, 'No, it is *mine*.' "[4] In the broadest sense, then, property law is an expression of control over the natural world. It is a language for deciding who owns what. And yet it is not a language that everyone benefits from equally. Nor is it one that can be counted on to master nature, in all its complexity, 100 percent.

Now if property is founded on possession and if modern technology makes it easier to control and thus to possess nature, then certainly this development must have affected the meaning of ownership. At some level, the law of property brings with it a vision of what nature is and to what degree it can be controlled. Some such vision was first worked out when the basis of modern Anglo-American property law emerged in England during the Middle Ages. When the colonists journeyed to America they packed the common law of property in among their cultural baggage. But what happened when this old and revered institution confronted a physical environment that was, as the colonists' descendants moved into the twentieth century, more thoroughly mastered than ever before? What kinds of dilemmas did the growing ability to control nature raise for a culture wedded to private property?

With such questions in mind I headed for the archives, where hidden in dusty legal treatises, buried in the case law, are some important lessons. There is a saying among lawyers that hard cases make bad law.[5] But do they make compelling history? The chapters that follow deal with such proverbial hard cases. If we want to understand how property law works to control the natural world, it is the difficult cases at the margins that have the most to teach us. To this end, the book consists of a handful of closely related legal stories. My approach is episodic—the gradual unfolding of a perspective—and thus I will not offer a comprehensive history of ownership or a linear argument that progresses chapter by chapter. Nor are these stories held out as typical or representative (if such stories even exist, which I doubt). They are meant instead to be emblematic and suggestive, to, above all, raise questions about the limits of private property in its ongoing and changing dialogue with the earth. The law is one of the strongest instances of institutionalized power in the world. My concern is to examine what happened when, in the modern era, property law sought to extend its powerful grip over the complex domain of nature.

[8]

There is a tendency to see the law as a force that exists over and above society, a hermetic discipline walled off from the rest of what goes on in nonlegal life. But in truth, the law of property penetrates everywhere in the realm of daily affairs. It is, for example, deeply implicated in our sense of place. It is there for the farmer plowing his fields, land he knows belongs to him because of some papers filed safely away in the county registry. It is there when he leaves home, with hammer and wire in hand, to go mend his fences. The law of property is there in the suburbs, in the hedges and picket fences that mark off the land, in the neatly manicured lawns that divide one property from another, there for all of us in the gates and railings we must negotiate every day. It makes no sense to separate the law and place it in a special hermetic category—the concern merely of lawyers, clerks, and judges—when legal concepts and assumptions are so thoroughly entrenched in our daily interactions with the environment. We need to ask what role the law of property plays not just in the courts but also on the ground, to see what it meant, say, for Indians along a river, farmers in a desert, oil companies on a lake, as they all deployed legal doctrine to control the natural world.

This book begins on the ground in the stunning Blackbird Hills of Nebraska, near the Missouri River. There we examine how white farmers wound up with three thousand acres of Indian land that disappeared from a Nebraska reservation. Is all land, even land along the shifting shores of the Missouri, suitable for ownership? Next we travel south to Louisiana to ask why it mattered that competent lawyers could not decide what makes a lake different from a stream (chap. 2). A silly question? Not really, since the answer would determine who owned a stretch of oil-rich land bordering the hard-to-define body of water. This story also

helps us examine the consequences of dividing the complicated world of nature into neat legal categories. Then the
setting shifts to regions above and below the earth's surface.
In Arizona's Sonoran Desert (chap. 3), we investigate who
owns the underground and its precious store of water. The
focus is on the ecological and moral consequences of ownership. Then we head back across the country to see who
claimed the weather in southern Pennsylvania (chap. 4) and
the air in New York City (chap. 5).

In the broadest sense, this book explores the dilemmas
of living in a culture in which the natural world has been
everywhere, relentlessly, transformed into property. The
American penchant for owning nature shows in one specific
and enormously important way how absurd and contradictory life in the modern world has become. There is no denying the whimsy and confusion of a culture that has tried
to impose capitalist logic on the seemingly nonideological
matter-in-motion we call nature. My point ultimately is that
the impulse to turn everything into property has not just
confused but impoverished our relationship with the natural
world by reducing that world in all its complexity into a giant
legal abstraction. The natural world's continual resistance
to human meddling suggests the weaknesses of a system of
thought that centers so thoroughly on possession. Moreover,
this impulse to transform nature into property may continue
to limit our ability to adapt successfully to the physical environment. A culture so single-minded in its pursuit of
property, especially private property, may sacrifice what
one anthropologist has called its "evolutionary flexibility"
and thereby foreclose on other ways (ways possibly more equitable and ecologically sustainable) of relating to the
earth.[6]

THE WORD *PROPERTY* has a complicated history. Today most people tend to think of property as a thing—a plot of land, a house, a car, or whatever. But this understanding of the word is not what English-speaking people always had in mind.[7] "In ordinary English usage, at least through the seventeenth century," writes C. B. Macpherson, "it was well understood that property was a right in something."[8] The something need not be a material object. A man could have property in a piece of land, but he could also have it in his life and in his liberties. For such people, the word had a much broader meaning than it does now.

What accounts for the difference? To start with, the vast majority of property under feudalism was in land, but unlike today, people did not have exclusive title to it. It was thus possible for several individuals to hold property rights in the same piece of land. At the bottom of the feudal hierarchy, for example, a tenant farmed the land; above him were various lords and barons who might have a claim to that same soil; and then, of course, came the king, who also had rights in the parcel. It would not do to refer to a piece of land as one's property when the land had a number of legitimate and competing claimants. Nor did medieval lawyers speak of people *owning* the land. Instead, the operative verb was *to hold*. Freeholders were, as the name suggests, holders of the land for a specified period of time. They did not own it as we might understand today.[9]

Under feudalism there were various obligations and restrictions governing how property could be passed along, as well as all sorts of dues and fines that tied up the land. But as capitalism began to develop, the meaning of property started to change. With the transformation of land into a commodity, with the emergence, that is, of a free market in land, it became possible to convey exclusive rights to real estate. More and more, people began thinking that what was changing hands was not so much the *right* to the ground on which they stood but the very land itself. "Limited and not always saleable rights *in* things," as Macpherson puts it, "were being replaced by virtually unlimited and saleable rights *to* things."[10]

Helping to speed property along this path was the development in the seventeenth century of mathematical surveying. Before this time, most English surveyors were unable to measure land accurately, especially irregularly shaped parcels. They lacked the necessary instruments and the basic knowledge. Many believed that a field containing a hill held the same area as an identical but flat field. Better training and tools, however, allowed seventeenth-century surveyors to produce much more reliable maps.[11] Land came to be seen as a thing having exact and measurable boundaries, an object of precise statistical quantity that could be sold, like pots or horses, for an equally definite price.

If you look up *property* in the *Oxford English Dictionary*, the world's authority on English usage, you will find that it is not until the eighteenth century that the word comes to signify "a piece of land." Now pull another volume of the *OED* off the shelf and find the closely related word *estate*. As early as the fifteenth century and probably before, estate meant the interest or right that one had in land.[12] But in the eighteenth century, precisely at the time when property begins to change its meaning, estate comes to denote a thing: "a landed property; usually, one of considerable extent," as in, "the rich families . . . retire to their estates."[13] The serpentine world of language and meaning shows how property was more and more coming to signify not a right but a thing—the thing we know today as land.

Nowhere did the idea of this thing called property garner as much attention as it did in eighteenth-century Britain. There a rich assortment of common rights—to graze cattle on pasture; to cut turf, chop timber, shoot game—fell victim to a new capitalist logic. The new logic put an end to shared rights in the land and in its natural wealth, pushing aside earlier communitarian claims in the name of exclusive possession. Traditional "commons" areas disappeared. A far more rigid set of boundaries founded on private property now cut across the earth; those who transgressed them did so at their own peril. To what lengths some people were willing to go to defend their property is made amply clear by the passage in 1723 of Britain's notorious Black Act. For such seemingly trivial offenses as stalking deer in forests with one's face blacked in disguise, for poaching hares, cutting down trees, and maiming cattle, the act prescribed no less a penalty than death. Designed in part to protect the security of landed estates, the Black Act signified property's status not just as a thing but as a thing in desperate need of protection. In *Whigs and Hunters*, E. P. Thompson explains the consequences of imagining property in this new way. "Since property was a thing, it became possible to define offences as crimes against things, rather than as injuries to men. This enabled the law to assume, with its robes, the postures of impartiality: it was neutral as between every degree of man, and defended only the inviolability of the ownership of things."[14]

Later in the eighteenth century, the famous legal scholar William Blackstone summarized the advent of a new era. "There is nothing which so generally strikes the imagination, and engages the affections of mankind, as the right of property; or that sole and despotic dominion which one man claims and exercises over the external things of the world, in total exclusion of the right of any other individual in the universe."[15] So it was that property became, in a word, fetishized. One can scarcely overestimate the enormity of the shift when property, previously conceived of as a right "in" something, assumes its new identity as the thing itself. Karl Marx talked about "the fetishism of commodities," the idea that the commodity, which in its origins and circulation had embodied a set of definite social relations among people, appeared instead to the human eye as simply a thing.[16] If we could ever figure out precisely how this transformation occurred, how social relations became somehow invisible when property redefined itself in the guise of things, then surely we would hold the key to understanding life under capitalism. It is clear that property had assumed some such fetishized form. Gone was the world of social relations. Property—land—was now merely a thing, pure and simple, offering itself to the world as a disembodied object in need of protection, legal and otherwise, to be bought, traded, and sold in the marketplace like so many pounds of cheese.

In this changed world, who could possibly quibble with the need to protect such discrete and valuable things? Certainly not America's own eighteenth-century revolutionary leaders, men as enamored of property as their conservative counterparts overseas. For Thomas Jefferson, the right to own land is what gave men the freedom to pursue happiness. It was landownership—not so much the right to the land as the actual possession—that defined his vision of the good society, a world made up of independent citizens secure in their individual property and thus dedicated to personal and social freedom. Own and be happy and free was his view. Indeed, it was Jefferson, not surprisingly, who dreamed up a plan to divide the entire Northwest Territories into neat little boxes. The boxes became the U.S. rectangular survey, which eventually imposed the grid system on some one billion acres—the better to sell and own them.[17] Even Tom Paine, a man given to radical ideas, had a special fondness for property, believing that, like liberty, the ownership of land was a natural right that should remain inviolate.[18] "In the young republic," William Scott remarks, "land and property were almost synonymous terms."[19] And both, people at the time felt, needed to be protected. "The stripping of forests to build fortifications around personal property," observed a London newspaper in 1780, "is a perfect example of the way those people in the New World live and think."[20]

After the fortifications came more than a century of fierce economic development. Capitalism evolved into its industrial phase as new forms of wealth and ownership began to appear—railroads, factories, corporations—and land started to recede somewhat in economic importance. Indeed, by the twentieth century, the near equivalence between land and property began to loosen somewhat as people recognized how many different kinds of property were now available to be owned. There were stocks, bonds, and various kinds of commercial paper. There were patents, copyrights, trademarks, franchises, and other types of intellectual property.[21] There was even something called the "new property," property that no one ever had dreamed was property, like welfare entitlements.[22] These forms of property were not truly things. They were abstractions. No longer did property simply correspond to something that one could plow or fence. This was a world wholly unlike the medieval one in which property signified rights rather than things. Things, even big and abstract things like corporations, now underlie the complex modern thinking about property. No wonder law students today learn, in what is perhaps the reigning property metaphor, that when they think of property they need to summon to mind a bundle of sticks—sticks of varying lengths and dimensions that can be sold one at a time, now or in the future, that can be taken away by the government if the public welfare demands it, that if necessary can be broken apart to serve the needs of transacting business in the global market, sticks that do not really exist.[23]

We have come a long way from the eighteenth-century understanding of property as land or estate or things. Blackstone's definition of property as absolute dominion over things has been replaced in the twentieth century by a more "dephysicalized" conception. Property, wrote one legal scholar in 1922, no longer describes any "object of sense, at all, and has become merely a bundle of legal relations—rights, powers, privileges, immunities."[24] Indeed, the increasing abstraction and complexity of modern economic transactions has led some to conclude that property, drained of its eighteenth-century "thinghood," has literally disintegrated.[25] Property in twentieth-century America has ended, so they say, another terminus to put alongside the end of ideology, of nature, and of history, about which social critics have had so much to say. It is popular today to proclaim the end of almost everything. In my own view, however, the American obsession with thing-based and land-based property is hardly over, even if the concept of property has grown increasingly vague and complex.

The ownership of land, for example, is still deeply embedded in the American way of relating to nature. Land has taken on new meaning in a culture where property, because it is so often abstract and dephysicalized, seems to offer its owners far less in the way of control. Consider what it means to own stock in, say, General Motors. Do shareholders own the company's factories? Not really. GM's board of directors can sell these factories or even go into an entirely different line of business, and an individual shareholder might exercise little direct control over the decision.[26] The increasing abstraction of modern property, in other words, has come at the expense of control over what one owns. Real estate in the twentieth century has consequently taken on new meaning. In a modern world of stocks, bonds, and intangible property, real estate is one thing over which property owners still can maintain absolute, direct, hands-on control. Hence the often intense opposition to environmental regulations limiting landowners' property rights.

Thus there is an understandable tendency to misconstrue real estate as the one real and solid property in a world where most other forms of ownership have shaded into abstraction. But it must be said that the law of real property itself has also grown more abstract and complicated. As we will see, however, increasingly complex legal doctrines have served to make more and more of the earth available to be owned. Clifford Geertz has written that the law is not so much a "set of norms, rules, principles, values, or whatever . . . but part of a distinctive manner of imagining the real."[27] Nowhere is that more true than in the realm of real property law.[28] Property law has, in effect, helped us to reimagine and reinvent what we understand to be the real world.

The following chapters investigate the kinds of distinctive problems that emerge when nature is fashioned as a thing that can be owned. Our task is to look into the world of possession, to dip into the web of social and environmental interdependencies bound up in what it means to own this planet. What we find, I believe, is that in modern America property has achieved almost transcendental status. Less and less of the physical world around us seems beyond the scope and influence of this institution. We worship property. Indeed it may be the only ecumenical passion left after the demise of patriotism. Further, we see the worship of property as a way of relating to the natural world so absolute and commonsensical that little can possibly escape its power. This book shows that if one pushes property law to its limits, what appears on the surface to be commonsensical is absurd, contradictory, at times even arrogant and destructive. The limits of the informal but widespread passion for property worship might suggest the need for a different form of reverence.

Certainly among the more problematic notions informing modern ideas of property is the belief that all land should have an owner. This notion is based on an economic logic that holds that the earth is put to its best use when a person claims it. This view is rarely stated explicitly, in part because it is so basic, so essential to a culture founded on property, that it rarely needs saying. Yet it is a view that most Americans subscribe to. It is an idea one is likely to encounter not only among realtors but also among members of the Nature Conservancy or the Audubon Society. I am not suggesting that Americans should burn their deeds and let the earth revert to an ownerless state. Instead, the chapters that follow show the limits to and consequences of owning this planet. Property law transforms nature into ownable things. But not everything on earth is equally ownable.

Herman Melville wrote in *Moby-Dick* (1851) that the world of property is like the ocean. According to him, maritime law and custom recognize only two kinds of fish: fast ones and loose ones. Fast-Fish belong to those who claim and possess them; Loose-Fish are free for anyone to catch and to own. So, too, with the world beyond the seas. How remarkable, Melville seems to be saying, that the whole world had come to be divided into the legal categories of fast and loose property. Writing from a vantage point in the nineteenth century, he satirized a system of thought in which possession was the only law. In this realm of the fast and loose, Melville asks, "What is the Archbishop of Savesoul's income of £100,000 seized from the scant bread and cheese of hundreds of thousands of broken-backed laborers (all sure of heaven without any of Savesoul's help) what is that globular 100,000 but a Fast-Fish? What are the Duke of Dunder's hereditary towns and hamlets but Fast-Fish? What to that redoubted harpooneer, John Bull, is poor Ireland, but a Fast-Fish?" Alternately, "What was America in 1492 but a Loose-Fish, in which Columbus struck the Spanish standard by way of waifing it for his royal master and mistress? What was Poland to the Czar? What Greece to the Turk? What India to England? . . . All Loose-Fish."[29]

But Melville's satire on the lust for property can be pushed one step further. As Mark Twain might have said, Show me a fast fish and I'll show you a fish that is a lot looser than you think.

1

Blackbird's Ghost: Real Estate and Other Fantasies

All lands should have an owner.
—U.S. SUPREME COURT (1890)

Leave it to the people at Walt Disney to come up with a good fantasy. In the 1968 movie *Blackbeard's Ghost,* a bunch of gangsters plot to take over an inn owned by some nice old ladies. The inn, located on an island off the Carolina coast, was once on the mainland, but a flood separated the property, leaving its ownership in limbo. Taking advantage of the whimsy of nature, the gangsters planned to open a casino there, until, that is, the ghost of the pirate Blackbeard appeared—intent on saving the inn on the old ladies' behalf. The entire story is pure Disney fantasy. Or is it?

If you look to the west of the Carolinas and pinpoint the ninety-sixth meridian, following it north through Texas, then straight through Tulsa, Oklahoma, you will notice that not long after it comes barreling into Iowa, it skirts just to the east of the little town of Onawa, home of the "widest Main Street in the U.S.A." Slightly to the left of that point toward the Missouri River is some land that has done so much traveling over the years that its ownership remains little more than a Hollywood fantasy.

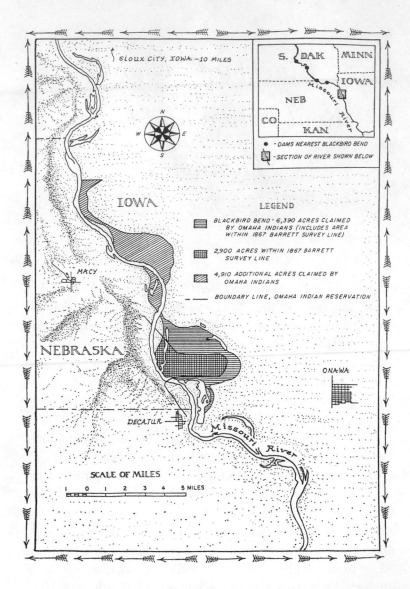

SCALE OF MILES

1 0 1 2 3 4 5 MILES

BLACKBIRD BEND AND VICINITY

Blackbird Bend is a thumb of land along the Missouri River. Only God knows who owns it; then again, maybe not. If the land could speak, what would it say? That once it was inhabited by the Omaha Indians. Then the Missouri changed course and land that had been west of the river ended up on the eastern bank, several thousand acres gone from the Indians' Nebraska reservation. Sometime early in the twentieth century it came into the hands of white owners in Iowa. Tiring of white ownership, however, the Indians decided to reclaim the land in 1973. About twenty of them trudged to Blackbird Bend in sneakers and blue jeans at about the time the Lakota, not too far away, were winding up their occupation at Wounded Knee. But no one remembers Blackbird Bend, except the Omaha Indians, of course. In 1975, the Indians occupied the land for a second time. Then the lawsuits began, a decade and a half of court appearances, motions, briefs, trial, and appeal. And still the most difficult question you can ask anyone along this brief stretch of Missouri Valley is only four words long: Who owns Blackbird Bend?

This question only matters to a culture determined to own nature, a culture of property. What I mean by this phrase is, very simply, a society that organizes its relations with the world, the natural world in particular, around the concept of ownership. Such a culture is so dedicated to control, so obsessed with possession, that it is willing to deny the complexities of nature to satisfy its craving to own. It is a culture lost in a fantasy world, a society that has long dealt with nature through the American dream of property ownership.

One of the greatest changes that ever took place in North America began with the arrival of the concept of private property sometime in the seventeenth century. Since that time, Americans have pushed their way across the continent on a mission of conquest, leaving millions of miles of fences trailing across the land—stone walls, wooden railings, barbed wire—with one main message to deliver: It is mine, not thine, so keep out. But every once in a while there comes a piece of earth that just will not fit neatly into the square hole of property. As we peer into that hole and study the history of Blackbird Bend, we are bound to learn something about a culture that can control nature, yes, but cannot control itself—one just desperate to own every last acre there is to be owned.

BLACKBIRD BEND takes its name from Chief Blackbird. He along with the rest of the Omaha Indians hunted there and across a huge expanse between the Platte and Big Sioux rivers. They moved into that area, it is believed, sometime in the seventeenth century. In the summer of 1804, Lewis and Clark ventured through the region. The explorers journeyed up the Missouri River, and when they arrived it was too late to meet Blackbird, who had died in a smallpox epidemic. According to Lewis and Clark, the Omaha "rove principally," which is to say that they hunted game such as buffalo, deer, and beaver. They also cultivated corn, beans, and melons. As far as the explorers could tell, the Omaha had "no idea of exclusive possession of soil."[1] That was to change soon enough.

It was the Omaha's supreme misfortune to be occupying prime agricultural land, property that white settlers yearned to have and to own. Through a series of treaties, the Omaha were gradually dispossessed of their land on the Great Plains. In 1820, the Indians gave up a small parcel so that the government could build a military post. Ten years later, they ceded control over land east of the Mis-

souri—what is now Iowa—in return for annuities. Another
ten years and the annuities ran out.[2] In 1854, broke and
weakened by attacks carried out by neighboring Indians,
the Omaha came to Washington to sign yet another treaty.
This one transferred rights to a huge expanse of land west
of the Missouri, about thirty-eight million acres in all. In
return the Omaha were allowed to keep a small parcel for a
reservation.[3]

The boundary lines laid out in the treaties hardly mattered to the Omaha, at least not in the way that they did for
the whites, who swore by the line. Even after the Omaha
ceded land to the government in the 1830s, they continued
to roam through the region in search of buffalo and other
game, transgressing precisely the same lines they had
agreed to on paper.[4] When referring to the land, the whites
spoke about meridians, parallels, and other landmarks.
Only a culture dedicated to owning the land exclusively
would use such a language, one that the Omaha were just
then learning to speak. With the treaty of 1854, the Omaha
were running out of land to cede. Three hundred thousand
acres including the land at Blackbird Bend was all that was
left of the Indians' once magnificent territory. Surrounded
by white people and their lines, they were expected to stay
put even if the lines themselves did not. Those boundaries
had a way of changing every now and then, especially the
reservation's eastern one, which the 1854 treaty designated
as the Missouri River.[5]

Exactly how the Omaha Indians felt about private property we may never know. But if the Omaha were to partic-
ipate fully in the culture of property, they needed to own
land. Only the 1854 treaty did not make the Indians landowners; it simply provided for the survey and allotment of
the reservation into individual parcels. If the U.S. govern-

ment chose to do so, it could remove the Omaha from their land, force them off to some more distant and perhaps less congenial place. No deed or other paper said anything to the contrary.

Then in 1882, Congress passed the Omaha Allotment Act. The act gave the head of each household one hundred sixty acres to be held in trust for twenty-five years, after which time the Indians would be issued a patent declaring them the owners.[6] It was a bill designed to educate the Omaha in the culture of property, providing more than a generation's time for them to learn the ways of that culture.

No one played a bigger role in this education than a Boston anthropologist named Alice Fletcher. In 1881, just five years after George Armstrong Custer and his men were massacred at Little Bighorn, Fletcher bravely journeyed out to the plains to study the Omaha. Fearless and determined, Fletcher was also evidently quite convincing when she chose to be. One colleague had this to say about her: "Some of her opponents never were quite sure what quiet, deep river had just drifted along and left them stranded far from their selfish hopes." Another observer offered this less charitable remark: She was a "dreadfully opinionated woman."[7]

Fletcher was in her forties when she went to the plains. When she arrived, she discovered that the Omaha Indians, quite unlike the white settlers she knew, considered themselves to be "a part of nature." The Indian felt deep down, she believed, that "no aspect of nature is clearly defined from his own life." It was a far less arrogant stance toward the natural world than that of the whites. It was also a philosophy that Fletcher was willing to do just about anything to change. Such a view of nature, she remarked, "is not conducive to . . . holding land as property, of placing a money value upon it, and passing it from one buyer to another as one would a garment." Indeed, since the Indians believed that everyone depended on the earth to survive, they wondered, according to Fletcher, how "one person [could] own land to the exclusion of other men." They did not wonder long. Because in Fletcher's opinion there was only one way for the Indians to succeed in the world—the white person's world, that is—and that was for them to embrace private property. So she shepherded the allotment act through Congress; then she personally educated the Omaha in the law of property so they too could become landowners and get on with the conquest of the continent. "Our laws of property and legal descent . . . ," she wrote tellingly, "were difficult to make clear to the comprehension of the people, owing to ancient tribal customs."[8]

Finally the day Fletcher was waiting for arrived. Early in the twentieth century, after the trust period ended, patents were issued giving the Indians title to the land. Now they were landowners, free to do what they wished with their property. For many, the first thing they did was put it up for sale. They had to in order to pay the debts they had accumulated and in some instances been tricked to embrace. When Fletcher revisited the Omaha in 1910, even she admitted the allotment act's failure, although she saw it more as a temporary setback, an inevitable adjustment to the equally inevitable world of property. In 1930, one of the most famous anthropologists ever, Margaret Mead, paid the Omaha a visit. Granting the Omaha fee patents, she later wrote, "exposed them to every type of attack by the land sharks who were assembling on all sides."[9] By the thirties, two-thirds of the land allotted to the Omaha had ended up in the hands of white owners.[10]

Gone too by that time was the land at Blackbird Bend.

The white man took it, just as he had the rest of the land, but not through some scheme or fraud. No shady-eyed brokers wheeling and dealing. The land at Blackbird Bend was gone all right. Several thousand acres vanished from the Omaha's Nebraska reservation and reemerged across the way in Iowa where white farmers were more than happy to have it. And claim it they did.

How did several thousand acres of Indian land disappear? The answer to that question can be found hundreds of miles northwest of Blackbird Bend in the town of Three Forks, Montana. That is where the Missouri River begins. From there it travels nearly one thousand miles, working its way through the Montana plains, picking up the Teton, Marias, Judith, Musselshell, and Milk rivers, before reaching a size that is likely to impress the wayward traveler. Then the mighty Yellowstone empties its full force into the river, carrying tons and tons of silt that it gathered up while coursing through the barren foothills of Wyoming. In North Dakota, the Missouri begins to angle south. Its waters swell even more as the Little Missouri, Heart, Cannonball, Grand, Moreau, Cheyenne, White, Niobrara, and Big Sioux rivers tumble in. By the time it reaches Blackbird Bend, if not before, the river has earned itself a name: the Big Muddy. The Omaha call it Ni-shu-da, or Smoky Waters.

The Missouri is the longest river in the United States. And it travels an unpredictable course as it etches its way through a watershed composed of loose, alluvial soil, the kind that at places crumbles like brown sugar into the river. With no solid land or rock to confine it, the river is always on the move, threading its way back and forth through a valley that is at points ten miles wide from bluff to bluff. Throughout its long history, the river has been everywhere in this huge valley. But there is also another reason the Missouri is so ready to shift course. This serpent of a river carries a huge amount of sediment that comes pouring off the arid, barren plains. It transports so much sediment that the writer George Fitch remarked in 1907, "Throw a man into the Missouri and he will not often drown. It is more likely that he will break his leg."[11] To handle all the material washed into it, the Missouri flows sinuously, since it can carry more sediment that way than by charting a straight course. Coiling back and forth across the land, the Missouri loops downstream, struggling to contain all the residuum of the Great Plains. At Blackbird Bend the sediment load has reached as high as three hundred acre-feet per day. In other words, on a daily basis, three hundred acres of soil one foot deep pass by this bend in the river—enough for a small farm. And the river swings across the plains, ready to move in whichever direction it must to deliver this load downstream.

So it is not hard to imagine the Missouri making off with Blackbird Bend. If the river—the reservation's eastern boundary—shifted a mile or so to the west, it would cut straight through the Omaha reservation. Alternatively, the Missouri could have just as easily swallowed up the land a little at a time, depositing it on the Iowa side. Either way, the Indians would lose. And as so often happened, the Indians' loss was the white man's gain—one man, Joe Kirk, in particular.

If it is hard to say exactly how the Omaha lost their land at Blackbird Bend—and the story, we shall see, is not a simple one—there is no question that by about 1916, Kirk had gained possession. Kirk came from Tennessee, by way of Kansas, and settled in the Blackbird Bend area around 1911. By the twenties, he had built a log cabin on the land, and there are some old black-and-white photographs to prove it. Another photograph shows a group of people posing in a watermelon patch that Kirk had planted out on the property. But mostly Kirk used the land to grow alfalfa to feed his livestock. During the depression, he rented it to tenants who cleared and farmed small portions.

To improve the value of the land, Kirk built levees during the thirties to help fend off the wandering Missouri. He also had some help from the U.S. government. By 1943, having tired of the Missouri's tendency to inundate the region, the Corps of Engineers and the Bureau of Reclamation—the two federal agencies in the dam-building business—set forth plans to control the waters of the valley. Unable to decide which plan to approve, Congress bested itself and adopted *both* projects. Lewis Pick, chief of the regional office in Omaha, was the author of the corps' plan. He summed up his main philosophy in one simple directive: "I want control of the Missouri River!"[12] Control is precisely what he got. In 1919, there were at least eighteen dams in the Missouri valley able to impound a total of a little more than one and a half million acre-feet of water. By 1974, there were one hundred sixteen dams; together they had the capacity to control over eighty-eight million acre-feet. That is more than twenty-eight trillion gallons of water, enough water to flood the entire nation of Poland to a depth of one foot. The biggest of these dams were built on the main stem of the river, huge structures hundreds of feet high. The dams flooded so much land that nine hundred Indian families in the Dakotas were forced from their homes.[13] But for white owners like Kirk, the dam building had a far more salutary effect. The dams, combined with the hundreds of miles of levees built by the government, stabilized their property, turning Blackbird Bend into a prime piece of real estate.

In 1948, Kirk and his wife, Bertha, put their land at Blackbird Bend up for sale. A good many lives became tied up in the property thereafter. The Kirks sold to Henry and Raymond Peterson, the Petersons to Messrs. Pace and Bookstrom, who in 1959 sold to Charles Lakin, a wealthy farm operator and land speculator. Living disproof of the old adage about death and taxes, Lakin managed to escape paying any property tax on the land until 1969, when the state of Iowa finally discovered the parcel and put it on the tax rolls. In 1972, Lakin sold to Roy Tibbals Wilson, who was in the cash register business and had learned about the property while traveling through the area. And cash register is an apt metaphor for how Wilson saw the property. He bought it to rent out to tenants at a profit. There was only one problem with this plan: The Indians said Wilson did not own the land.

IN APRIL 1973, the Omaha Indians headed off to Wilson's land to reconquer it for their people. More than a hundred years had passed since the Omaha had settled on the reservation, and it looked as beautiful as it always had, still a world of rolling hills, green and brown shading off toward the horizon. But a closer look revealed signs of suffering: old and sagging farmhouses, shingles falling off, broken-down Fords, population and average income in 1970 exactly the same number: sixteen hundred.[14] Escaping this troubled world, the Indians arrived at Blackbird Bend. By the time they got there, Wilson had retired somewhere in Florida, having long since rented out the property to be farmed. The Indians pitched a fifteen-foot tepee and two tents. They brought along a tractor for picking corn and a big pile of wood to ward off the chill of night out on the plains. They also carried with them one other thing: a large framed copy of their 1854 treaty with the U.S. government. The document, so the Indians said, proved their claim to the property.[15] As far as the occupation went, there was none of the spectacle of Wounded Knee. None of the bloodshed either, although the manager of Wilson's land claimed that he was chased off and later told he would be shot if he returned. No hostages, FBI agents, or federal marshals. Just twenty-some Indians trying to reclaim what they believed to be rightfully theirs.

Their leader was Eddie Cline. Cline came from a long line of leaders. Both grandfathers and his father served on the Omaha Tribal Council, the tribe's governing body, and so did Cline himself at various times in his life. He first recalled seeing Blackbird Bend while traveling on horseback as a child. But not until 1962 did he discover from old records and maps that Blackbird Bend belonged to him and his people. "The U.S. government laid down on the law," Cline later said. "As far as the tribe is concerned, the U.S. government as a guardian of our lands let this property get away from us."[16] So when the government failed to act, Cline decided to take matters into his own hands. By the time of the occupation, he was in his forties, and he was acting on his own authority since he no longer served on the tribal council. While Cline and his followers were on the land, they fished, cut down a fence, and dug up a drainage pipe to block access to the area. A month later, Cline was arrested. He was charged with stealing corn from the property. The charges were later dropped, but an injunction keeping the Indians off the land was issued.

History repeated itself two years later when Cline and the Indians returned to the property.[17] Not long before, Cline had been reelected to the tribal council. That mattered because the injunction had been based on his not representing the tribe in an official capacity. "That was all Indian land over there," said Clifford Wolfe, Sr., a member of the tribal council, sometime later. "We think about our children and our grandchildren. From the income, maybe they'll feel like we're people. Maybe it'll help their schooling, give them something to fall back on. We want that back. Any way we can get it back, we want it back."[18]

The U.S. government, convinced of the legitimacy of their claim, was willing to help the Indians. With Cline and others still in possession of the land, it filed a suit on behalf of the Omaha claiming title to twenty-two hundred acres at Blackbird Bend. So that the Indians could remain on the property while the suit went forward, the government moved for a preliminary injunction to keep the white owners off. It was a clever idea. With the Indians in possession, the government argued that such an injunction maintained the status quo ante, however brief it might have been. And best of all for the Indians, the strategy worked.

For decades the only Indians allowed on Blackbird Bend were the ones sent out there to work it for the benefit of its white owners. Now the Indians were back in possession of the elusive property, at least for the moment. They farmed the land and put the proceeds in an escrow account pending the outcome of the lawsuit. The account built up but not at a rate that satisfied the land's former owners. Blackbird Bend was prime agricultural land, some of the most fertile soil in the country. There could be only one explanation, reasoned the white owners, for the land's present poor performance: the Indians just did not know how to farm it. Otis Peterson, once a tenant farmer at Blackbird Bend, now stood by and observed the Indians who had put him off the property. From what he could tell, the Indians were doing a poor job: "I can only say that the crop of weeds will be excellent."[19] The conclusion to be derived was clear: What they could not properly farm, they could not properly possess, or so the white owners told the judge.

If the argument sounds familiar, it is because it has been used for centuries to justify the culture of property. Travel back in time to the seventeenth century and you will find that the New England colonists, for example, tapped it to deprive the Indians of their land. Either improve the land or lose it, went the logic there. Or as the minister John Cotton once put it, "In a vacant soyle hee that taketh possession of it, and bestoweth culture and husbandry upon it, his Right it is."[20] It was a long way from the world of John Cotton to that of Wilson and the others out on the Iowa plains. Yet such a philosophy still held a good deal of credence nearly four centuries later. Only in this case, there was little doubt that the Omaha were improving the land, though admittedly not as fast as the whites would have liked. So the judge in the Blackbird Bend matter refused to return the property to the whites.

It was a move Harold Sorenson just could not believe. Sorenson's parents came from Denmark all the way to Miller, South Dakota, to bust the sod and plant flax. In 1939, Sorenson and his wife, Luea, moved from there to Onawa and purchased about a hundred acres.[21] Blackbird Bend was still littered with brush and cottonwoods in those days, and Sorenson and his family cleared it by hand. Later on, when he first heard about the Indians and their land dilemma, he sympathized. He signed a petition saying they should be given back their land. He allowed them to cross his property—tepee, tents, framed treaty, and all—on their way to occupy Blackbird Bend in 1973. Then he learned that some of his own land might be Indian property. He closed the road that the Indians had been using. "I think that ruling is the most unbelievable part of the whole deal," Sorenson said about the judge's decision to let the Indians remain in possession. "It was like me coming up to you and saying, 'I own your house,' and then having a judge say I can go ahead and move in while we settle who owns it. Isn't that a mess?"[22] It was an interesting analogy, in part because it highlights one of the guiding principles of the culture of property in contemporary America, that nature and houses are equally ownable. Put up some fences and no trespassing signs and the land is as much yours as the two-story farmhouse that you build on it.

Is private property as rock solid as Sorenson's remark suggests? An answer can be found in the struggle that developed over this peripatetic piece of land. After the government filed its case, the Indians, believing that the government had failed to adequately pursue their cause, hired a lawyer and launched some lawsuits of their own. The most important of these alleged title to more than sixty-three hundred acres at Blackbird Bend—over four thousand more than the U.S. government claimed—as well as additional land upstream from Onawa. All told, the Indians claimed title to over eleven thousand acres, plus fifty million dollars in damages. By the late seventies, the Omaha, who had once controlled a sprawling expanse of land on the northern Great Plains, now owned a mere twelve thousand acres. Success in their lawsuit would nearly double the tribe's land base. But reclaiming Blackbird Bend meant more than just land and money. Somewhere in that land the Indians hoped to recover not just soil and water but the very identity of the Omaha people. "Without land we're not a people, and we're not people without land," explained Doran Morris, whose great-grandfather Yellow Smoke had signed the 1854 treaty.[23] Willard Phillips, an Omaha leader, put it this way:

"A man put out a book that says 'Know your roots.' That's what I say. If you don't know your lifeline you ain't nobody. And that's what I want for my kids."[24] That and a few thousand acres of land across the river in Iowa.

Eleven thousand acres of land might not sound like that much to ask for. But for Vincent Willey, an Iowa farmer whose family had been on land now claimed by the Indians for some four generations, it was not the land so much as the principle that mattered most. "If my dad killed somebody, if my granddaddy killed an Indian, does that mean I have to pay for it? Sure there are some things not to be proud of. Naturally we took the whole country from 'em. But are we all gonna pack up and go back where we came from?" Look into the eyes of any of the white owners in Iowa and you would find an answer to that question. Willey only worried about what would happen if they lost. "Some of 'em," he said, referring to the other Iowa landowners, "you'd carry off in coffins."[25]

ONCE A HUGE COTTONWOOD TREE over four feet in diameter stood at Blackbird Bend. When cut down in the 1970s, it was said to be sixty-seven years old. The cottonwood is commonly found in this region, and the Omaha once used it to make the Sacred Pole, a symbol of tribal identity associated with buffalo hunting. With the decline of the buffalo in the 1870s, the Sacred Pole disappeared from the tribe's ceremonial life, the last one carried off in 1888 to Harvard's Peabody Museum to bear testament to a fallen culture.[26] Meanwhile, white settlers on the plains had found a new use for the cottonwood. The Timber Culture Act of 1873 gave title to one hundred sixty acres to settlers who planted trees on forty of them. Since the cottonwood grew fast and needed little care, it was a favored tree in this enterprise; William Least Heat-Moon recently called it "the mortgage tree" for this reason.[27]

The cottonwood grew closer to the world of property and real estate when the Omaha decided to stake their claim to Blackbird Bend on it. To see why the Indians chose to do so, we ourselves must delve further into that world to explore how it handles the dilemmas imposed by the chaos of nature.

Lawyers turn out to be excellent accountants as well; they have rules for deciding what should happen when water adds or subtracts from a piece of real estate. Foremost among these is the rule of accretion. It says that soil that accumulates gradually and imperceptibly along rivers, lakes, and seas is the property of the adjacent owner. Property boundaries shift outward with the addition of new land. The rule has roots in Roman times, but it was most clearly articulated in Britain. Small additions of land are of no use to anyone but the adjoining owner, a British case from 1828 explains. So the custom was to allow title to such inconsequential amounts of property to change hands. "Much land which would remain for years, perhaps for ever, barren," the case reads, "is in consequence of this custom rendered productive."[28]

Perhaps the rule made sense in a place like England where additions to land bordering water were nominal (mostly because rivers meandered only modest amounts there and more often flowed in beds made of solid rock). Venture across the Atlantic to the similar terrain of New England and still there was little to object to in the rule. But would the doctrine of accretion apply as it headed west to tackle the tumultuous world of the Missouri? No less an authority than the U.S. Supreme Court said that it would hold there as well. "All lands should have an owner," the court wrote in 1890, and accretion served this end admirably.[29] Of course, the quantity of land involved in this part of the world could amount to hundreds, even thousands, of acres.[30] Not only that, in the twentieth century, courts in the Missouri valley have applied the rule to man-made changes, so long as the landowner himself was not chiefly responsible for creating the new soil.[31]

Accretion seeks to maximize the productive value of nature. Let the natural world change and property boundaries too would shift to take advantage of nature's new potential. But suppose the change is not gradual and imperceptible, the standard for proving accretion. Suppose instead that a river makes a sudden and noticeable departure. The law has a remedy for this situation as well, the rule of avulsion. This rule also tries to capitalize on nature's economic potential. Should there be a sudden and presumably massive shift in natural conditions, no landowner could feel secure in his property unless the law enforced the status quo ante. Avulsion is set up to do precisely that. It is a rule that favors the past, the way things were before nature disrupted the property. And in keeping with that reasoning, ownership of the displaced land does not change hands.[32]

Accretion and avulsion are static legal categories for describing what should happen when nature intrudes on the world of property relations. They are neat and ideal stories that the law tells about the natural world. Yet neither story, of course, can remotely capture all the complexities of river movement on the Great Plains. Neither is nuanced or sophisticated enough to render legible and clear the dynamic world of nature. Neither has the precision or power for reading a natural world that is messy and unable at times to be read. But these stories would be told there on the plains nonetheless.

The Blackbird Bend trial opened at a little after one o'clock on November 1, 1976, Judge Bogue presiding. Andrew Wendell Bogue was fifty-seven when the trial started and an old man before the matter was anywhere near resolution. He had been scheduled to try the Indians accused of murdering two FBI agents at Wounded Knee. Instead, he was handed the Blackbird Bend case.[33] The trial itself lasted a little more than one month and involved extensive testimony as well as a field trip—Bogue with a group of lawyers in tow all tramping out to Blackbird Bend for a look. The trial transcript fills twenty-one volumes and runs to exactly 3,214 pages. So many papers were filed in the case that an entire room in the Sioux City courthouse is devoted to the matter. Of Judge Bogue, one lawyer asked to evaluate his honor's judicial temperament wrote simply, "Great man."[34] He had to be to endure this case, one that refused to go away, that stuck to his docket like Blackbird Bend mud to his shoes.

William Veeder was the lawyer for the Omaha. He once described himself as "basically a conservative person," although few people today would agree.[35] In his opinion, the Omaha's troubles began on March 5, 1496, not one day before or after. On that day, Henry VII, King of England, commissioned John Cabot to go in search of "provinces or regions hitherto unseen by Christian people." What Cabot started, Lewis and Clark plus a stream of white settlers, now lost to history, finished. The result was clear to Veeder: "Genesis of the present grave problem of the Omaha Indian Nation and the Indian people comprising that Nation, can be attributed directly to avidity to occupy, without right, the lands of the Indians."[36]

The trial concerned about twenty-nine hundred acres. That number represented the amount of land within what was called the Barrett Survey, after Theodore H. Barrett who marked the easternmost limit of the Omaha reservation back in 1867. His line was the only solid one to be found in the chaos of land and water that was Blackbird Bend. All the remaining property claimed by the Indians would be dealt with later.

About this land Veeder had much to say. But for him and the others gathered in Judge Bogue's courtroom, only one thing mattered. Who owned Blackbird Bend would depend on how the Missouri River behaved in the time since the Omaha were granted their reservation in 1854. In other words, title to the property rested on the history—complex though it was—of land and water at Blackbird Bend.

The only Indian to testify at the trial was Eddie Cline.[37] He explained how the Omaha had gone about occupying the land, but he had little knowledge about the Missouri's effect on Blackbird Bend, the main issue at the trial. So Veeder had to rely on a number of expert witnesses to make his case. Of these, perhaps the most important was Charles Robinson—geologist, engineer, charter member of the Association for Professional Geological Scientists, and an expert on rivers and sediments. Robinson noted that in 1867, when Barrett first surveyed Blackbird Bend, it was a thumb of land that protruded into the Missouri River. Over the next eight years the thumb grew. As the river entered the bend, water near the surface flowed faster than water at the bottom of the river. Centrifugal force then came into play. It imparted a circular motion such that each particle of water traveled downstream like the thread on the surface of a screw. The result was that water closer to the surface bit into the concave bank eroding it; water lower down took the material and added it to the convex (Nebraska) side of the river.

Slowly the river moved to the east, carrying more and more soil to the Nebraska side. Blackbird Bend grew bigger.[38]

The Indians were profiting, briefly reversing the process started by Cabot, when all of a sudden, sometime between 1875 and 1879, the river moved to the west, cutting them off from the land the government had granted in 1854. According to Robinson, when the river reached a certain point in its eastward migration, it tried to move south but was stopped by a deposit of clay not prone to erosion. So it moved suddenly westward instead. An avulsion took place, in Robinson's words, "a sudden, an abrupt change of a river from one channel to another." And since there is no change of ownership with an avulsion, the land, Veeder argued, still belonged to the Omaha.

For the next three decades, the river migrated slowly to the north and Blackbird Bend once more expanded in size. Then came another avulsion. The only witness the tribe could find to prove it was the lone cottonwood tree mentioned earlier. A little computation explains what happened. Subtract the tree's age of sixty-seven from 1976, the year it was cut down, and you arrive at its date of birth, 1909. Since the tree started growing before 1912—the earliest the river could have suddenly shifted course—and still existed after this time, an avulsion must have taken place, reasoned Veeder. Had the river eroded land by moving slowly to the south, it would have swept the young tree away. But if the river moved *suddenly* in that direction, it would have left the cottonwood intact—there to bear witness to an avulsive change, to the fact that the land was still Indian property.

The tribe's case came down then to these two sudden periods of river movement. After the 1920s, of course, man-made influences became more strongly felt at Blackbird Bend, as Veeder and the tribe were well aware. Kirk built levees; the corps constructed dikes and other means of water control. The impact of this work was twofold: it trained the Missouri to stay within a designated channel, and it also caused land to slowly accrete to the Iowa side of the river. As this was happening, Kirk and others moved onto the land and, in Veeder's estimation at least, "got rich on it."

Veeder and the tribe had one story to tell about Blackbird Bend; the white owners, of course, had another. Lawyers for Wilson and the other defendants went in search of a witness with enough authority to refute the tribes' claims, someone who would weave an entirely different tale about this embattled piece of property. In Raymond Huber they found their man. It took a good part of a morning for Huber to set forth his credentials to the court. Born in Kansas City, Missouri, in 1907, Huber had gone to work for the Corps of Engineers at age eighteen. He had been trained as a civil engineer. For almost four decades, Huber devoted his life to one thing: the control of nature. The corps put him in charge of stabilizing the Missouri's channel all the way from Rulo, Nebraska, in the state's southeastern corner, to Three Forks, Montana. By his own account, he visited Blackbird Bend no less than three hundred times, by boat, car, and plane and on foot. When he finally retired in 1963, Huber was awarded one of the corps' highest honors: the Meritorious Award for Outstanding Civilian Service. ("This award," he told the court, "consists of a medal which I can attach to ribbon, which I can wear around my neck, and also a pin for the lapel.")

Did he have an opinion about what happened at Blackbird Bend between 1855 and 1890? Yes, he did. It "gradually eroded westward, and as it did erode westward deposition in the form of sand and accretion was formed" on the Iowa side.

Did he have an opinion about the period from 1906 to 1923 (little evidence existed for the intervening time)? Yes. The river eroded the reservation, "and deposition occurred to the east, Iowa shore."

Was there any evidence of avulsion between 1923 and 1940? None.

Could any of the structures the corps used to control the river have caused an avulsion to take place? "No, sir."

It was not that Huber's view of what happened at Blackbird Bend was in its details all that different from the tribe's story. Both sides, after all, were using largely the same evidence—mostly maps and surveys—to reach their conclusions. What was different was Huber's—and the defense's—understanding of *avulsion*. As Huber understood the word, it involved the transfer of a "piece of land from one bank of the river to the other" such "that you can follow the movement of that transfer of land and identify it as the identical land which formerly existed on the other bank, beyond any power of question." Now that was an exceedingly narrow definition of the term, far narrower than the one offered by Robinson and the tribe ("a sudden, an abrupt change of a river from one channel to another"). Using such a strict standard, one could argue, precisely as the defense did, that no avulsion whatsoever had taken place.

Not only had no avulsion taken place but, according to the defense, the tribe's own people supported that conclusion. They pointed to a series of letters written between 1906 and 1917, roughly the time when the tribe postulated an avulsion. The letters were indeed written on behalf of the Omaha people, Indians who found that their allotted lands were being destroyed by the Missouri River and who were asking the U.S. government for a new piece of property. Dora Pappan, for example, found that of the forty acres of corn her son-in-law planted near the Missouri, only six were left, "the remainder having been washed away." There was no mention made of any sudden, avulsive shift, just water slowly eroding the land.

If any of the Indians mentioned in the letters were still alive, not a single one came forth to testify at the trial. The closest either side in the case came to an eyewitness of river movement was George W. Prichard. He was eighty-two when he took the stand and had lived in Onawa for the last three-quarters of a century. In his younger years, Prichard and his father often set off with a pack of hounds to hunt cows and rabbits near Blackbird Bend. "Particularly cows. My father liked to chase them." In the summer of 1919, about the time of the avulsion asserted by the tribe, Prichard met Joe Kirk, saddled up some horses, and headed out to the area. All morning they rode, Kirk telling him his plans for the newly created property. Did Prichard see any indication of land cut off from the Nebraska side of the river while out there? No. Was there any indication of land other than new land that had slowly accreted to the Iowa side? None.

More witnesses were called than there is space to tell here. Then on December 6, 1976, the trial finally ended. In many ways, the history of what happened at Blackbird Bend remained as complex, muddled, and inconclusive as ever. History, one scholar has lately observed, is "a series of messes."[39] It certainly looked that way at Blackbird Bend.

Bogue pondered the evidence for six months before issuing his ruling. "During the period from 1854 until at least the early 1940s," he wrote in an introduction to the opinion, "the Missouri River can best be described as in a wild and uncontrolled state."[40] To a people obsessed with the control of nature, those may well have seemed like sensible words. But it is just as easily argued that what is *wild* is the effort to pour tens of thousands of tons of concrete and steel into keeping the river from charting its own course toward the sea. The control of nature is one thing; but the nature of control, to turn things around, is that it has limits.

Bogue then went on to give a detailed analysis of river movement between 1855 and 1940. Everywhere he looked he saw accretion. He dismissed the sixty-seven-year-old cottonwood, holding that the tribe rested its case that the tree proved avulsion on questionable assumptions about where the river had actually been at different times in the past. He found fault with the credentials of the tribe's experts (one, a surveyor, he pointed out, was "neither a geologist nor a hydrologist"). Certainly none of the tribe's experts could possibly match Huber's thirty-seven-year record on the Missouri. He also thought it "somewhat strange" that the river would move east and north by accretion and in the opposite directions "by a 'jumping action' so as to qualify in the eyes of the law as an avulsion."[41] And most important, Bogue rejected the tribe's understanding of avulsion. Instead, he opted for the narrower definition offered by the defense, that identifiable "land in place" needed to be shown to prove it. That definition virtually guaranteed that Bogue would find accretion—a ruling, it must be said, that favored society's possessors, particularly those with land along the river who stood to benefit from the slow addition of new soil. So impressed was Bogue with the defense's theories that when he sat down to write his thirty-five-page opinion, he took all but six of those pages directly from a pleading filed by the defendants themselves—verbatim.

"We thought all along he would rule against us," said Eddie Cline afterward. "I guess the only surprise was that he really had the audacity to follow through and do it."[42] So Cline and the others refused to budge from Blackbird Bend. Three times in May 1977 the county sheriff and his deputies came out to the property to put the Omaha off. Three times they were turned away.[43] The Omaha had a sign up at the edge of the land. It said

BOUNDARY LINE

OMAHA INDIAN RESERVATION

NO TRESPASSING

They meant it.

On May 13, 1977, just as the Indians were being offered one last chance to leave, a messenger arrived. He brought word that a federal appeals court said the Omaha could stay until it ruled on Bogue's decision.[44] Almost one year later, the appeals court overruled Bogue.[45] It pointed to an old federal law that said that in a trial over property between an Indian and a white person, the burden of proof rests on the white so long as the Indian can demonstrate "a presumption of title in himself from the fact of previous possession or ownership."[46] Such a presumption was simple enough for the Omaha to prove; all anyone need do was look at the 1854 treaty. The ruling increased the burden of proof on the defendants. Meanwhile, the court also made it easier for the tribe to prove an avulsion by broadening Bogue's definition of that term. An avulsion, the court explained, involved "a sudden perceptible shift of the channel." The case law said so, precisely as the tribe had argued. "We hold the evidence too conjectural and the ultimate conclusion reached too speculative to sustain the defendants' burden of proof," concluded the court.[47] Title to twenty-two hundred acres, the court ordered, belonged to the tribe. But a small fraction of all the land the Omaha claimed, it was something nonetheless.

For more than a decade, the case moved up and down through the federal court system on appeal until a decision was finally reached on who owned the remaining seven hundred acres at Blackbird Bend. Although the reasoning need not detain us, title came to rest with the non-Indian owners. And the same held for all the remaining land—some eight thousand additional acres—claimed by the Omaha on the Iowa side of the river.[48] "The Indians want everything the Missouri River ever touched," said Don Ruth, an Iowa landowner, "but that just isn't the way it is."[49]

The court of appeals' 1978 ruling cost Harold Sorenson some land at Blackbird Bend but not nearly as much as Roy Tibbals Wilson, who said good-bye to more than one thousand acres. Wilson was understandably upset. "Why wouldn't I be upset?" he told one reporter after the decision. "It wasn't the right ruling. It's like somebody coming to my house and saying, 'You get out of here because we're going to take over.'"[50]

ON THE LAND that once belonged to Wilson and others, the Omaha have decided to build a gambling casino—thirty thousand square feet of blackjack, poker, and dice. The property seems well situated for such pursuits. Doran Morris, now tribal chairman, explains that in building the casino, the Omaha are trying to forget the past problems that arose over Blackbird Bend. "That was yesterday, now we're

going on," he explains. "Now we need employment, my
people are poor. And this is how we will do it."[51] Some, like
Harold Sorenson, find it difficult to forgive and forget. Sorenson refuses to give the casino his business. "I can just
see some night a guy in a big Cadillac with Kansas City
plates rolls in here and wants to know where the casino is."[52]

Sorenson, like Wilson, had compared the loss of land at
Blackbird Bend to the taking of his house. How did both
men come to imagine the land in this way? In part, of
course, it has something to do with the assumptions of a
culture that by this point in the twentieth century had grown
used to having its way with the natural world. Blackbird
Bend exists today, if it exists at all, because of the technological domination of nature, transformed by the Corps of
Engineers, among others, into a *thing* that can be owned.
Moreover, this aggressive stance toward nature has been incorporated into the language of property. Consider the
thoughts of Jeremy Waldron, who teaches law at the University of California at Berkeley, some seventeen hundred
miles away from Blackbird Bend. "In a system of private
property," he wrote recently, "the rules governing access to
and control of material resources are organized around the
idea that resources are on the whole separate objects each
assigned and therefore belonging to some particular individual."[53] By implication, nature under such a system is a
resource, a simple utility destined to be controlled and manipulated to serve largely economic ends. And like all other
resources in the private property system, nature must also
be divided up and treated as a set of "separate objects" or
things. The culture of property strives to imagine the natural world in such a way so as to control, dominate, and own
it. Nature is thus broken apart so it can be put back together
as individual pieces of property. But things were not so sim-

ple at Blackbird Bend, where the river fought back and
reassigned property rights.[54]

To imagine Blackbird Bend as a thing—such as a
house—is to picture it in isolation from the world. It is in
some sense to lie, to hide from view the social and ecological relations of owning land in this place. Nobody built
Blackbird Bend in the same way one did a house, and nobody can own it in quite the same way either. Yet the house
analogy is powerful precisely because it expresses a sense
of entitlement while at the same moment obscuring the assumptions on which that entitlement rests. For the white
owners to envision the land as a house that they built meant
denying that it once belonged to the Omaha. It also involved
repressing the role that an uncontrolled Missouri played in
delivering the property into the hands of the white people.

If you took Blackbird Bend, overlooked the complexity of
the land there, and forgot about the Missouri River and the
sound of water washing against soil, you perhaps might end
up with a house or some other "separate object." Then put
a fence around the property, go inside, and close the door.
Now a group of Indians, from another state no less, come
knocking at that door, say the land is theirs, sue you, and
win. It might well seem to you, as it did to Sorenson and
Wilson, that someone had come right into your home and
taken it. But what Sorenson and Wilson really lost was
something they never had: absolute control over land in a
place where control of any sort is hard to fathom.

Property in land is an act of denial, a wish for closure,
for solid control and dominion over nature. Perhaps that explains why the law still refers to land as *real* property, to
deny what is unreal, porous, and imaginary about it. Yet as
real as property in land may seem, it is still, of course, a
legal fiction for imposing rational order on an often uncoop-

erative environment. Property law is the voice of reason that we use to tidy up the messy and dynamic world of nature. But take its rules for ordering nature far enough and you wind up eclipsing that reason altogether.

If you have any doubts, consider the following recent piece of unparalleled logic.

> OMAHA (AP)—Zigs and zags of the Missouri River could complicate attempts by a Nebraska Indian tribe to build a casino on tribal land in Iowa, officials said.
>
> The Omaha tribe of Macy wants to build a casino near Onawa, Iowa, about 60 miles north of Omaha.
>
> But changes over the years in the Missouri River channel might have put the Iowa tribal land within Nebraska borders, a deputy Iowa attorney general said.
>
> "The river no longer is necessarily the exact boundary," Sherie Barnett said. "It's a very complex legal squabble over who owns what."
>
> But Barnett also said state officials are confident that the tribe legally possesses land in Iowa.
>
> "Whether we all agree that they own the same piece of land, I don't know," Barnett said. "Hopefully the parcel that the Omahas ultimately choose to place their casino on will be something everyone can agree is actually in Iowa."
>
> If the tribe's land is considered to be in Nebraska, the tribe couldn't negotiate a

casino compact with Iowa, Barnett said.
Nebraska law prohibits casino gambling.

"To me, the tribe has a problem," said
Thomas R. Burke, an Omaha attorney who
has represented Iowa landowners in a
court battle with the Omaha tribe that began in the 1970s.

"They must be assuming that the land
is in Iowa, just because it's on the Iowa
side of the river."[55]

2

Identity Crisis
in Bayou Country

Until we become nomenclators of a place, we can never really enter it.
—WILLIAM LEAST HEAT-MOON (1991)

On January 27, 1964, Six Mile Lake became a stream. No act of God, no natural disaster, no work of man played a role in the lake's sudden transformation. What sounds like a shift of enormous ecological proportions was really the product of just a few men huddled together in a courtroom somewhere in Baton Rouge.

Six Mile Lake is in southern Louisiana's Atchafalaya basin. It is part of North America's largest river basin swamp, bigger even than the famed Okefenokee. As the sun arches up in the sky and the fog begins to lift, day settles in over bayou country, an aqueous, obscure world of twists and turns. Look down into the water and you will see reflected a battle-worn landscape studded with immense cypress stumps as much as ten feet in diameter. Those trees once towered one hundred feet above the land, the wood now lodged in a decaying cabin or coffin moldering in the ground somewhere. Death weighs heavily on the landscape, but then so does life. The Atchafalaya, home to hundreds of species of birds and fish, is just brimming with wildlife, with egrets swooping down gracefully over the water, with alligators lurking near to shore, with crawfish, shrimp, clams, mussels, mullet, and shad, with mink, nutria, ducks, turkeys, deer, and on and on, as if a host of Noah's arks descended on the swamp and opened their doors.

Imagine more than three-quarters of a million acres of such life and death, think for a moment about those twisting, mist-enveloped bayous, and you will soon understand the mix of beauty, terror, and mystery that surrounds this place. But of all the many mysteries one finds here, perhaps the most persistent concerns two bodies of water, Grand and Six Mile lakes. These are not average lakes. Some people had trouble believing that they were lakes at all. To the unbeliever they were something altogether different, rivers or streams maybe, but not, let me repeat, not lakes. Why, one might ask, should anyone care what name was used? Because a great deal of property and money rested on the name. For the law in Louisiana attached (and still attaches) great importance to the names given such bodies of water. How they were named would determine who owned them, a point of no small importance. Ever since the 1960s, landowners, oil companies, conservationists, and lawmakers have all been locked in battle over the Atchafalaya's future, a struggle that has hinged on how nature ought to be classified and named. Down in the delta, where the earth looks watery and the water earthy, where land and water come together in strange ways, it was to be no simple task to determine nature's identity. There is a great deal at stake— far more than one might think—in a name.

How does the language of property work to possess nature? What are the consequences of changing the natural world into property? How well can we capture nature, in all its fluidity and chaos, with a name? With such questions in mind, we venture below into the symbolic life of property.

THE ATCHAFALAYA is truly a modern river.[1] Born sometime around A.D. 1500, the point when historians say that history became—in a word—modern, the Atchafalaya grew to be the most important distributary (bayou) of the Mississippi River. The Mississippi itself has done a good deal of wandering in its day; it has changed course three times over the last fifteen hundred years. Sometime about five hundred years ago, a loop of the Mississippi meandered westward and broke into the Red River basin, giving birth in the process to the Atchafalaya. Modernity and hydrology came together for a brief moment.[2]

Placed as it was, the Atchafalaya soon became choked with logs, trees, and whatever else came pouring down the Red and Mississippi rivers. Near the head of the Atchafalaya, the debris piled up to form a raft that stretched downstream for roughly forty miles. But beginning in 1831, the raft stopped growing when channel changes were made upstream where the Atchafalaya, Red, and Mississippi rivers came together. Those changes stopped both debris and water from flowing downstream, causing the Atchafalaya to grow smaller. It is said that the Atchafalaya in 1839 could be crossed with the aid of a mere fifteen-foot plank. Barely more than three hundred years old, the Atchafalaya teetered on the verge of hydrological death.[3]

Then in 1840, the state of Louisiana began dismantling the river raft. It did so to improve water transportation between the Mississippi and the region farther west, rescuing the Atchafalaya's future in the process. The job of tearing apart the raft was not completed until 1861, but when it was done, the Atchafalaya was given new life as it now had the capacity to divert increasing amounts of water from the Mississippi to the Gulf of Mexico. Indeed, it became clear that, left to its own devices, the Atchafalaya would eventually capture the entire flow of the Mississippi, leaving Baton Rouge and New Orleans stuck in a tidal backwater. The way the numbers work, a trip down the Atchafalaya to the Gulf is roughly two hundred miles shorter than the same trip down the Mississippi. It seemed inevitable that without some kind of human intervention the Atchafalaya would assume a new identity as a reincarnated Mississippi River.

By the twentieth century, the Atchafalaya had gone from being a diminutive stream to a full-fledged distributary of the Mississippi. And it continued to enlarge, especially after the devastating 1927 flood, which drove over a quarter of a million people from their homes and inundated millions of acres of land.[4] The disaster prompted the federal government to pass flood control legislation in 1928 for the Mississippi valley. The U.S. Army Corps of Engineers then set off to tame the waters of the region. Building miles and miles of levees, dredging millions of cubic yards of earth, the corps tried to expand the carrying capacity of the Atchafalaya so that when the next flood struck, the river could be used to handle the Mississippi's overflow. Seeking to address the need for flood control, while also wary of the Atchafalaya's tendency to run off with the entire Mississippi River, the corps had its hands full, dredging here, building there. Over the course of several decades, the corps gave the entire land- and waterscape a massive reworking, a tremendous face-lift that sketched out a new identity for the Atchafalaya.

But in 1952 there came a prediction that left the corps anxiously scratching its collective head. According to a

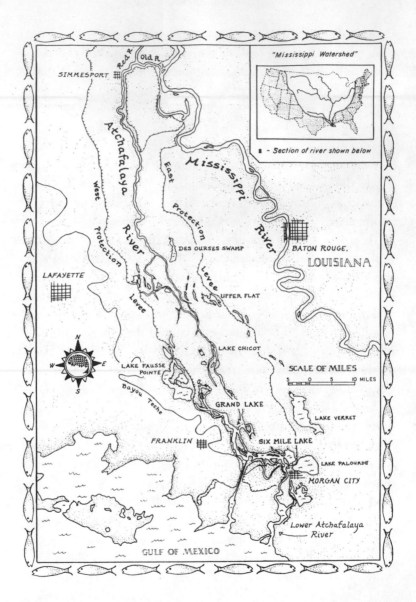

ATCHAFALAYA BASIN

study prepared by the corps itself, sometime before 1975 the Atchafalaya would become the new route for the Mississippi River. With no time to lose, the corps started building structures to forestall that eventuality. In the meantime, roughly 25 percent of the yearly flow of the Mississippi was going down the Atchafalaya, and that number would grow higher during the 1950s.[5] But more than just water was washing down the Atchafalaya. With the water came whatever sediment happened to be in the river at the time. The amount of such sediment was hardly inconsequential, not with the Mississippi River basin draining 41 percent of the continental United States plus two Canadian provinces for a total of over a million square miles. A Kansas farmer who threw seed on his land before a heavy rain was likely never to see that seed again, nor for that matter was his counterpart in Iowa or Nebraska who did the same. For that seed and more was headed south to bayou country where it would either settle or flow out to the Gulf of Mexico. Tons and tons of silt and sediment found its way into the Atchafalaya basin, especially after the 1930s when the federal government finished an extensive dredging project that carved a single channel forty feet deep through the river above Grand Lake. The newly dredged channel increased the amount of water and silt that now coursed into the lower part of the Atchafalaya basin.

That water, loaded with the remains of the Mississippi watershed, then made its way to Grand and Six Mile lakes. Together, the lakes acted as a vast stilling basin. As the water moved through the lakes, they slowly filled up with silt. Between 1930 and 1952, more than sixty square miles of new land appeared within the lake, so much land that one could now rightly wonder whether the name "lake" made any sense at all. The average sediment load passing by

Simmesport, Louisiana, at the head of the Atchafalaya, was more than a quarter of a million tons per day between 1964 and 1974.[6] That is a lot of material, enough to make these lakes slowly vanish in a single lifetime. Seventy-eight-year-old Alcide Verret, who still hunted squirrels for his breakfast in 1979, had this to say about the changing nature of the Atchafalaya basin.

Lord, how this swamp has changed! Years back I could stand on the shore of Grand Lake and barely see across to the other shore. Just open water. Why that lake was so big they had to have lights to guide the boats. Now it ain't nothing but willer bars and silt. All these young people are crying, "Save the Atchafalaya." Hell, ain't nothing left to save![7]

The Atchafalaya River may well be a modern river. But beginning in the 1930s, it started to undergo a fundamentally postmodern experience—a crisis of meaning and identity. It looked much like a river might for its first hundred miles or so. Then the trouble began as the river approached what some now called "the Grand–Six Mile Lake segment." Before the dredging done in the thirties, the river, for roughly fifty miles north of Grand Lake, had dispersed into many small, shallow streams that ultimately emptied into the lake. With the dredging of a single channel through this area, the nature of this part of the river changed, and so did the look of Grand and Six Mile lakes. What were once termed lakes were by the middle decades of the twentieth century hardly so any longer. The Corps of Engineers had worked a massive disappearing act, a vast series of manipulations that had stolen the identity of this part of the basin right from under it.

Meanwhile, the culture within the basin was changing as

well. By the twenties, in what was once the heart of a multi-million-dollar lumber industry, loggers were cutting the last of the region's red cypress.[8] With the cypress swamps now cut over, entrepreneurs had nowhere left to go but down, beneath the now barren land to the oil and gas reserves below. The discovery of oil in the swamps along Bayou Teche early in the twentieth century brought oilmen and their companies into Louisiana, eager, calculating, and full of hope as they drilled down into the earth. The search paid off, and by the thirties, Louisiana ranked as one of the most productive oil-producing states in the nation. There was oil under Grand and Six Mile lakes, or what was left of them, and some of America's biggest corporations—Gulf, Texaco, Amerada, and others—wanted to own and profit from it. The problem was that the oil lay beneath an uncertain terrain, under land that was slowly emerging as silt poured down from the north. It was by no means clear who owned the newly created land and the oil below. The oil boom and the fast-changing land- and waterscape had combined to bring oil companies and private landowners into a struggle with the state over who had the legal right to the lucrative property.

That struggle was mainly over how to name nature. The names inscribed on Louisiana's waterscape—put there by cartographers and explorers who had ventured through the region in the nineteenth century—produced nary a word of dissent or objection and would have continued along this peaceable path were it not for an obscure statute that lay buried in the Louisiana Civil Code. Article 509, enacted in 1870, reads in part, "The accretions, which are formed successively and imperceptibly to any soil situated on the shore of a river or other stream, are called alluvion." Title to the alluvion belonged to "the owner of the soil situated on the edge of the water.'"[9] Under the code, the legal meaning of alluvion seemed clear: accretions that had formed on the shores of *rivers and other streams*. Much less clear was what constituted such bodies of water. Article 509 thus raised the question of how water would be classified under the law. If Six Mile Lake was indeed a lake, then the statute would not apply and the state would retain title to the newly formed land. For no one disputed the state's title to the bottoms of all navigable waters, a property right that it held from 1812 when Louisiana joined the Union.[10] Otherwise, if Six Mile Lake was understood to be a river or stream, the oil companies and private landowners (from whom they leased land) would gain title to the new oil-rich property.

A lot more than just oil revenue was tied up in the identity of this water. Beginning in the sixties, as the Louisiana courts struggled to divide lakes from streams, the curtain went up on what would be a long battle over the Atchafalaya basin's future.[11] In 1963, the Corps of Engineers proposed enlarging the main channel of the Atchafalaya to neutralize the sedimentation problem and enhance the river's flood control capacity. That plan worried sportsmen and conservationists, who feared for the basin's fragile habitat. Later in the decade the Louisiana legislature endorsed the creation of a national recreation area to protect the region's environment. Yet the creation of any state or federally regulated area would hinge on wresting control of the basin away from private landowners along Six Mile Lake and elsewhere. Call it a lake and state coffers would jingle with the extra oil revenues, not to mention the control the state would have over the region's ecological destiny. Call it a stream and private landowners would experience a windfall, not just in oil but in the money the state would have to pay them should their land be taken by eminent domain.

"Tell me how you classify," wrote Roland Barthes, "and

I'll tell you who you are."[12] Barthes's point was that there are always great stakes involved in how things are ordered. With the Atchafalaya's "lakes" filling in with silt, their identities unclear, the Louisiana courts searched for the right nomenclature to describe the state's waterscape. And so did the parties in the legal cases that developed as they strove to answer something many had thought they had learned in grade school. What is a lake? turned out to be no simple question. For how did one set about proving the identity of a body of water, much less one that was in the process of disappearing?

SIX MILE LAKE became a stream in 1964; the decision in *State* v. *Cockrell* said so.[13] The case began five years before when the state of Louisiana and Gulf Oil Company, which leased mineral rights from the state, brought an action for trespass against Ernest Cockrell, Jr., a Texas oil entrepreneur, and the Southern Natural Gas Company. Cockrell had drilled an oil well near the southern shore of Six Mile Lake in 1959. The state claimed ownership of the land on which the well had been drilled, land it believed to be part of the bed of Six Mile Lake. The defendants, however, argued that the well had been drilled on alluvion. In their view, Six Mile Lake was a river or other stream under the meaning of article 509.

Prior to the court of appeal's decision, the case was tried before Judge E. L. Guidry in the district court of the Parish of St. Mary.[14] Witnesses began testifying in March 1960. There were many witnesses called to the stand, but by far the most important ones were the scientific experts employed by both sides to identify the body of water in question. The defendants' star witness in this regard was Reinhard Steinmayer.

Not just any old geologist but the man who founded Tu-

lane University's geology department in 1922, Reinhard
August Steinmayer cut a very impressive figure. He was
sixty-eight when the *Cockrell* trial began. A highly regarded
academician, a consulting geologist, and above all, an expert on sedimentation in lakes, Steinmayer was exactly the
man the defendants were looking for. When he was called
to testify, the defendants' lawyer, S. W. Plauche, wasted no
time in getting to the point. In the months that you spent
studying the Atchafalaya River basin, Plauche asked Steinmayer, did you reach an opinion on whether Grand–Six Mile
Lake was a lake or stream? Yes, indeed he had, replied
Steinmayer. That lake was a stream. The Grand–Six Mile
Lake segment, Steinmayer believed, was a "running body
of water." From this it followed "that the Atchafalaya
River—and I am referring now to the lake segment—is both
competent and has the capacity to transport and did transport a considerable amount of material." He had other reasons to support his conclusion. For example, he found that
a thalweg, or channel, existed in the area. Thalwegs apply
to running bodies of water, Steinmayer explained; he had
never heard the term used in connection with a lake. In
studying historical documents dating back to the eighteenth
century, Steinmayer discovered that the area in question
had maintained a "sinuous shape," again suggesting "that
it was formerly a running body of water that meandered in
its channel." He also noted that lakes have waves and deposits of peat on their bottoms, but he could find evidence
of neither in the Grand–Six Mile Lake segment. There
seemed to be no doubt about it: What Steinmayer had on
his hands was a stream.

That was not, however, a view shared by Leo Odom, who
testified for the plaintiffs. A civil engineer who had once
worked for the Corps of Engineers in New Orleans, Odom
believed the body of water in question was a bona fide lake.

From the outset of his testimony, Odom adopted a historical tack. He reviewed for the court what had happened in the Atchafalaya River basin over the last century or so. He explained how the discharge of the Atchafalaya had grown after 1839 as efforts were made to remove the river raft that blocked the progress of water downstream. He noted how in the 1930s the corps had excavated one hundred million cubic yards of earth over a fifty-mile span north of Grand Lake, causing more water and material to flow down into the lake area. But he also pointed out that whatever filling in had taken place, Six Mile Lake was still three miles wide and Grand Lake roughly eight miles at its widest point. In contrast, the Mississippi River at Baton Rouge was a mere two thousand feet across. Those statistics presumably proved that Grand–Six Mile Lake was a lake, at least if one took width to be what divides lakes from streams. Nor could he find any signs in the area of natural levees, the buildup that can occur where a stream flows into a lake, thus further supporting his contention. But he did, contrary to Steinmayer, find wave action, exactly as he expected of a lake. All of this added up to one inescapable conclusion: These bodies of water were just what their names said they were.

Of course, Plauche, the defendants' attorney, was unprepared to accept such a conclusion. In his cross-examination, he forced Odom to admit the presence of a substantial current in the water. There was no denying that fact. Then he tried to undermine Odom's point that a width of three or more miles was indicative of a lake. Citing from no less an authority than the *Times Atlas of the World*, Plauche administered a geography lesson.

PLAUCHE: The Hudson River, forty miles upstream from its mouth, at Bayonne, is three and a half miles wide. You apparently were not aware of that?

ODOM: That's right.

PLAUCHE: Is that right?

ODOM: I didn't know how wide it was. I know it has a wide place there in it.

PLAUCHE: You know it has a wide place up there? Do you know that the Delaware River, twenty-five miles upstream from Cohansey Creek to Delaware Strait, [is] two and one-half miles wide. Did you know that, sir?

ODOM: No.

Unimpressed by Odom, Judge Guidry, who delivered the district court's opinion in 1962, embraced Steinmayer's views instead. And it is no wonder that Guidry found Steinmayer more credible. For his testimony neatly matched what Guidry took to be the meaning of the words *lake* and *stream.* Where did Guidry turn to find the meaning of these words? To perhaps the most obvious place of all, the dictionary. Using a variety of law and other dictionaries, Guidry concluded "that the basic difference between a river or other stream and a lake is that, in the one case, the water has a natural motion or current, while in the other, the water in its natural state is substantially at rest, that is, without a perceptible flow."[15]

There one had it. In one body of water a current existed; in the other there was none to speak of. It was that simple. Steinmayer, of course, had discovered a running body of water. So had John P. McDowell, assistant professor of geology at Tulane University, who also testified. Odom had noted the presence of a current. Even the plaintiffs' own witnesses, Columbus Voisin and Ervin Anslum, men who had hunted and fished in the area, admitted the fact. There was indeed a current in that body of water, and what flowed—if you will forgive me—from this fact seemed clear to Judge

Guidry. "Regardless of the alleged facts and arguments advanced in support of the proposition that Six Mile Lake is a lake and not a stream, I am constrained to hold that it is a stream and not a lake in the technical sense of the law."[16]

For the moment, the decision stopped the plaintiffs from pursuing their cause. But it did not stop the silt that was rushing into the Atchafalaya basin from filling in what the law had now ruled to be a stream. Guidry's decision did not sit well with the state of Louisiana. It had much to lose if the decision stood—thousands of acres in the Atchafalaya basin, one of the country's most beautiful wetlands, not to mention lots of money in oil revenues. The plaintiffs felt that the lower court had simply adopted Steinmayer's views wholesale. Steinmayer, as the plaintiffs saw it, had relied largely "on the speed of water in Grand Lake . . . but he did not pretend to lay down a rule as to a 'speed limit' of water which results in the classification of a lake as a stream." If the waters in question were not lakes, wrote the plaintiffs on appeal, "then one must say there is just no such thing in Louisiana."[17] There were lakes, to be sure, in Louisiana. There just were not a lot of them that could be legally defined as such—at least that is one way of understanding the lower court's decision in *Cockrell.*

Cockrell was not the first time that the Louisiana court system had wrestled with the identity of a body of water. Similar questions had arisen in *State* v. *Erwin,* a case involving Calcasieu Lake in the extreme southwest corner of the state. Although the Calcasieu River flowed into and through the lake, the Supreme Court of Louisiana in 1931 ruled "such a vast expanse of water as Calcasieu Lake as being in fact a lake."[18] But the court cited no case law to support this conclusion, and thus the "vast expanse" rule lay open to criticism.[19]

The initial blow to *Erwin* came in 1943 with *Amerada Petroleum Corporation* v. *State Mineral Board*, or *First Amerada*. That case involved Arm of Grand Lake, a body of water west of Lake Chicot at Grand Lake's northern end. Citing the trial court's opinion, the supreme court held that a lake is a stagnant body of water without current. A river differed from a lake, the court continued, "in that it flows, more or less, in a permanent bed or channel between defined banks or walls with a current, whereas streams are bodies of flowing water including rivers."[20] Without explicitly overruling *Erwin*, the court shifted from an emphasis on physical dimensions to a focus on the current. And in 1946, the court reaffirmed this new standard in *Amerada Petroleum Corporation* v. *Case* (*Second Amerada*).[21]

When the state and Gulf Oil appealed the lower court's decision in *Cockrell*, these earlier cases were construed against them. The *Erwin* case had indeed been overruled, chiefly by *First Amerada*, concluded the court of appeal. It was the current, or lack thereof, the court believed, that mattered most in determining the identity of bodies of water. The court noted that Steinmayer, who based his view on both historical maps and personal observation, believed Six Mile Lake was a stream from before 1812 until the present. And the court agreed. Impressed, perhaps overly so, with Steinmayer and his testimony, the court found that Six Mile Lake had a current, that it had a thalweg or channel, that it lacked peat deposits, and that it once had natural levees—all the major signs of a stream.[22]

If one believed Steinmayer and the court, Six Mile Lake had long been a stream. But what evidence supported this conclusion? One person the court drew on for support was William Darby. Darby had ventured through the Atchafalaya basin in the early nineteenth century. In 1816, he published a map of Louisiana along with a "geographical description" of the state. There was little question that Darby observed a current in the Atchafalaya. Darby, the court noted, had written that "the rapidity of the current of the Atchafalaya, and the quantity of water drawn by its efflux from the Mississippi, is almost inconceivable."[23]

The court of appeal also mentioned the work of James Leander Cathcart. A few years after Darby published his work, Cathcart too journeyed to the Atchafalaya basin. A navy agent acting under the authority of the U.S. government, Cathcart went there in search of timber to build new military ships. While in Lake Chetimaches, the name then in use for Grand and Six Mile lakes, Cathcart observed a current of one mile per hour. The court of appeal then was able to show that a current existed in Six Mile Lake long ago, making it a stream under the law.[24]

A current may well have existed in the body of water back in the early nineteenth century. But did that alone make it a stream when Louisiana entered the Union in 1812? What should be made of the fact that Cathcart called the body of water *Lake* Chetimaches, or that Darby used that same inscription on his map of the area? Lafon's map of 1805, Graham and Tanner's map (1834), Graham's map (1838), Bayley's map (1853), all submitted into evidence by one side or the other in the case, inscribe the water as a lake.[25] To be sure, the names given this area vary: Lake Chetimaches, Lake Sale, Grand Lake, Grand Lac, but a lake no less. It was not, however, the names on these maps that interested Steinmayer or the court of appeal. Mere names did not concern them. Their minds were fixed on the current, a feature that if present proved—according to Steinmayer and his scientific standards—that this body of water was a stream, despite what others in the past had chosen to call it.

All that was left standing between Steinmayer, the Louisiana courts, and total unanimity on what constituted lakes and streams was Judge G. Caldwell Herget, who dissented from the court of appeal's decision.[26] Steinmayer, Herget seemed to say, could believe whatever he wished about lakes and streams. What was important was the "plain meaning" of such words. The Louisiana Civil Code itself advised that words were "to be understood in their most usual signification." When article 509 pertaining to alluvion was adopted, wrote Herget, all surveys and maps "alluded to the body of water herein involved as a lake." It appears illogical to me, he remarked, that "the Legislature intended to classify such body of water as a river or stream." "Indeed," he continued, "to accept the definition accorded to the word 'stream' by the majority would mean that the Atlantic Ocean through which the Gulf stream flows at a rapid rate and without question makes imperceptible accretions on the shores thereof is not in fact an ocean but a stream."[27] Surely nobody, not even the grand master of streams, Steinmayer himself, would be willing to go that far.

Perhaps better than anyone, Herget sensed that this case was a battle over meaning and interpretation. How was it possible to classify a body of water when there were so many different ways of investing that water with meaning? Meanings piled up, one upon the other, as cartographers, travelers, surveyors, and geologists all put forth their own ideas about what constituted a lake or stream. Sometimes those meanings overlapped to form some common ground. And sometimes they did not. But it is the history of those different meanings that may well be most important. For in that history lay a simple truth. None of the meanings given the words *lake* and *stream* adequately represented the body of water in question. In regard to classification, Michel Foucault once wrote, "We shall never succeed in defining a stable relation of contained to container."[28] Of course, that has never stopped anyone from trying.

ON JUNE 10, 1974, Six Mile Lake became a lake—again; or so ruled the Supreme Court of Louisiana in *State* v. *Placid Oil Company*.[29] The case had a very long history. In 1963, while the courts were still wrestling with *Cockrell*, the state of Louisiana and its lessee, Gulf Oil Company, filed another action for trespass, this time against Placid Oil and J. Ray McDermott & Company, another oil firm. The year before, the defendants in the suit had drilled three wells west of the Cockrell Well in Six Mile Lake. Over the next year, they produced more than half a million dollars worth of oil. The state was asking for the return of that money and, more important, that it be declared the owner of the property on which the wells had been drilled. The plaintiffs in this case were the same as in *Cockrell*, and although the defendants were different, the issues involved were largely the same. The stakes, however, were higher. As the case made its way through the courts, the debate over the future of the Atchafalaya began in earnest. By the end of the sixties, state sponsorship of a plan to turn part of the Atchafalaya swamp into a national recreation area focused attention on the newly created land along Six Mile Lake. It would save the state a whole lot of time and money if it already owned the new land, money that would fall directly into the hands of landowners and oil companies should they be declared in possession. So once again, the Louisiana courts struggled with the identity issue to see who would retain title to the oil-rich property.

The case was tried for three weeks in 1967 before Judge

Edward A. de la Houssaye III. Not until three years later did he make his decision. Ruling in favor of the defendants, he determined Six Mile Lake to be a stream in accordance with Louisiana law.[30]

Once again Reinhard Steinmayer made a court appearance and laid out the same familiar story about Six Mile Lake's status as a stream. Put simply, it was a running body of water that flowed in a channel and had the ability to transport sediments. Indeed, it had all the features that Steinmayer expected a stream to have. Historical documents—travelers' accounts and survey reports—noted the presence of a current. It meandered, a point Steinmayer developed by using a series of maps, laying them one upon the other. It sloped downstream and had a thalweg. It had a great discharge capacity as well as natural levees. It had no significant signs of any peat deposits. Moreover, no less an authority than the Corps of Engineers considered it a stream. Steinmayer noted that the corps had continuous *river* mileage figures for the Atchafalaya River. His point was that they did not break off the numbering when they reached the Grand–Six Mile Lake segment. Instead, they forged ahead, a full one hundred thirty-five miles from the start of the Atchafalaya River to the Gulf of Mexico.

Although he made a convincing witness, Steinmayer's testimony was not without its faults. Not long after taking the stand, Steinmayer made a slip of the tongue. The Corps of Engineers, he said, has considered Six Mile Lake to be "a lake—I mean, as a running body—correction—running body of water." Is it possible that deep down, somewhere in his unconscious, the indubitable Steinmayer felt a shadow of a doubt?

In need of a witness to match Steinmayer in expert ability, the plaintiffs this time chose Charles R. Kolb. A geologist employed by the Corps of Engineers since the 1940s, Kolb had helped to prepare one of the most important documents ever written on the Atchafalaya basin, *Geological Investigation of the Atchafalaya Basin and the Problem of Mississippi River Diversion.* That was the study published in 1952 that predicted the Atchafalaya would capture the Mississippi sometime before 1975. Well aware of what the corps had done in the way of dredging and other work in the basin, Kolb had some strong opinions of his own about the identity of the water in question. Relying on what the basic geological textbooks said, Kolb defined a lake as "a fairly sizeable body of water that occupies a depression in the earth." A lake, he added, "can have an outlet on one or more sides or it can be entirely closed." Under this definition, there seemed little question that to his eye, Six Mile Lake was exactly that, a lake.

Kolb thought Steinmayer was all wrong on the lake versus stream question. Steinmayer said a high volume of discharge flowing through a body of water indicated a stream. Kolb offered statistics to show that this was not always true.[31] Steinmayer believed the presence of a current suggested that Six Mile Lake was a stream. Kolb argued that currents could be present in both lakes and streams. Steinmayer attached great importance to the absence of peat deposits. Kolb argued that many large lakes in Louisiana had no peat in them at all. Steinmayer pointed to the corps' *river* mileage figures; Kolb called Steinmayer's point "presumptuous." And Kolb ought to have known, having worked for that institution for over two decades. On down the list Kolb went, offering in the end his own version of what constituted a lake. If Grand–Six Mile Lake was wider than the Atchafalaya River that entered it, which it was, if the current decreased as it flowed into Grand Lake, which it did, if average channel volume was diminishing, which it was (from the filling in of the lake area), and if the sediment load decreased in a downstream direction, which it did, then what you had, plain and simple, was a lake.

Judge de la Houssaye, however, had this to say about Kolb and his opinions: "The Court has carefully considered the testimony of Dr. Kolb, and finds that it is not entitled to much if indeed any weight." Kolb had erred in one very important regard. He had set forth his own standards of "lakeness," not those sanctioned by Louisiana law. Yet it was what Louisiana jurisprudence took to be a lake that counted. And under that law, as lately articulated in the *Cockrell* case, if a body of water had a current with the ability to form accretions, then it was a stream. In fact, Kolb himself had admitted the presence of a current, a substantial one, in Grand–Six Mile Lake. Kolb, as de la Houssaye noted, had tried to argue that the presence of a current was something that could be found in either a lake or a stream. "This may be," wrote the judge, "but in any case in Louisiana wherein this issue is raised, where the facts establish that a particular water body does have flowing currents of such power and velocity as to form accretions, then that water body is going to be judicially determined to be a stream until such time as the Supreme Court or the Legislature changes these criteria."[32] Case closed.

It would take another four years before the supreme court changed its mind. In the meantime, the plaintiffs appealed, only to lose again. Affirming de la Houssaye's decision, the court of appeal cited the earlier decisions in *First Amerada* and *Cockrell* to show that a body of water with a current capable of depositing soil was a stream under Louisiana law.[33]

Only Judge Paul B. Landry, Jr., chose to dissent from the opinion.[34] It was an odd—and some might say brave—dissent as Landry had been the author of the court's opinion in *Cockrell*. Much more impressed with Kolb's testimony than his colleagues on the court, Landry reviewed it to show how the basin had been manipulated by engineers and others over the last century or so. But what he wanted most, it seemed, was a return to the rule laid down in *Erwin*. To his mind, the "vast expanse" rule articulated in that case was still good law. As he put it, "large, expansive bodies of water, having relatively shallow channels and ill-defined banks, are characterized as 'lakes' notwithstanding a river or stream flows through it." Thirty miles long and three to ten miles wide, Grand–Six Mile Lake was in its "natural condition"—before, that is, the corps and others got through with it—"more characteristic of a lake than a stream."[35] In 1964, at the time of *Cockrell*, Landry had contemplated this same body of water. Then he thought he saw a stream. Now after eight more years of siltation, as Grand–Six Mile Lake was slowly disappearing, Landry looked again, reviewed the history of this body of water, and found it to be a lake. Or maybe that was just wishful thinking on his part.

Their plea rejected by the court of appeal, there was only one other place for the plaintiffs to turn in their struggle—the state's highest court, the Louisiana Supreme Court. With over one hundred thousand acres of property ultimately at issue, the stakes were high, the legal briefs voluminous. William Guste, the state attorney general, reminded the court "that it is the future of the Atchafalaya basin as a great wilderness that is at stake, one of the very few remaining in the State and in the country."[36] That future hung in wait as the court tried to sort out what kind of water body this really was. It was hardly an easy job, and when it was all over there would still be no unanimity.[37]

The opinion in the narrow four-to-three decision was written in 1973 by Judge Walter F. Marcus. He saw it as the court's task to determine the identity of Grand–Six Mile Lake when Louisiana entered the Union in 1812. In making this determination, Marcus felt that the rule laid down in *Erwin*—holding a "vast expanse" of water to be a lake— was "unworkable and arbitrary." "The use of such a standard," as he put it, "would make it next to impossible to determine when a water body was wide enough to be classified as a lake and narrow enough to be considered a river or stream."[38] And in any event, he continued, *Erwin* had been overruled by *First Amerada*, which established the presence of a current capable of forming accretions as the standard. Legal precedent and scientific evidence, mostly that of Steinmayer, suggested that the court of appeal be affirmed, or so thought Marcus and the others who joined him in the ruling.

To Judge Mack E. Barham, however, the majority opinion was not merely wrong. It was nothing short of foolish, not to mention "catastrophic" in its effect "upon the public fisc, our natural resources, our ecology, our environment, and the public in general." Barham was stunned by what his colleagues on the court had done. "The majority has decided that these cases," he wrote, referring to the earlier court decisions on lake classification, "force a conclusion that a lake is not necessarily a lake, that a lake may be a river or stream." Humbug, he thought. "Amazingly, the majority has said, oh, of course, Grand Lake is not a river (a large body of water) it is a stream (a very small running riverlet or creek). It is impossible for my mind to conclude that a body of water, which is as much as 30 miles in length and 10 miles in width, is a mere stream or riverlet." For his mind and lots of others we might suppose. Not a geologist, a hydrologist, or any sort of scientist for that matter, Barham could nonetheless say what constituted a lake. And he could say it forcefully.

I am of the opinion that lakes may exist even though they have current consistently in a portion of their confines. I am of the opinion that lakes exist even when rivers or streams source them and empty them continuously. I am of the opinion that the geological information about velocity, capacity, power, force and thalweg, do not change a lake into a stream.[39]

But say what he would, Barham alone could not change the majority ruling. Although two of his fellow jurists, Albert Tate and Pascal Calogero, joined him in dissenting, the rule still stood: If it had a current and could carry silt, it was for all legal intents and purposes a stream.

Defeated once again, the plaintiffs marched back to their briefs and in a last-ditch effort forced a rehearing of the case. The briefs continued to pile up, including one especially worth noting, by W. Scott Wilkinson on behalf of the Placid Oil Company, a defendant in the suit. Wilkinson took issue with Barham's dissent in the original hearing. As he understood it, Barham was "saying that the name of a water body determines its characteristics and the laws applicable to it." Wilkinson knew better, or thought he did. "This is just the reverse of good logic, because in all things it is the nature and characteristics of a thing that determine what it is. From all of its parts we determine what a thing is."[40]

If it were only that simple. What Wilkinson overlooked was the enormous economic and political stakes involved in the case. Never mind that if the area in question were declared a stream, Dow Chemical Company would gain tremendously at the state's expense, having filed a similar suit alleging title to over fifty thousand acres of the former Grand Lake. Never mind that while the court was reconsidering the matter, Louisiana's governor, Edwin Edwards, raised the political stakes by declaring the newly formed land at issue part of a state wildlife refuge. One newspaper called Edwards's action "an empty gesture."[41] But it was, in fact, a solid indication that the governor wanted the body of water to be pronounced a lake.

No doubt such matters were on the judges' minds when they reheard the case. As it turned out, the new opinion, issued by Chief Justice Joe Sanders, overruled *Cockrell*, the earlier *Placid* decisions, and Reinhard Steinmayer and his views on lakes. According to Sanders, the court had been mistaken in two respects. It had erred in holding that *First Amerada* had overruled *Erwin*, and it had given "undue weight" to the presence of a current in classifying water bodies. How then would the state's judiciary proceed on the matter of classification? The court elected a more pluralistic route, supporting a "multiple-factor test." Size (especially the width of the stream), depth, banks, channel, current, and last but not least, "its historical designation in official documents" were all to be considered. Such a standard had at least one virtue: It attached some importance to how the water had been named. The decision can be understood to mean that names really do matter. With the new multiple-factor test, Grand–Six Mile Lake became a lake again under the law. Its physical features suggested such a classification, and so did the fact that from early on it had "been designated on official maps as a lake."[42]

More than anyone, it was Justice Sanders who sealed the state's victory. When he first heard the case in 1973, Sanders ruled the water a stream; six months later, he changed his mind. Some years before the ruling, Sanders wrote in an article entitled "The Anatomy of Proof in Civil Actions" that justice depended on "the best fact finding" our judicial system could offer.[43] The facts for him were out there in the world; all judges and juries need do was discover them. But Sanders's flip-flop on the lake versus stream question suggests that, on the contrary, legal facts are not discovered but created.[44] Moreover, his ambivalence in the case embodies the very indeterminacy of trying to neatly classify the natural world.

As the water slipped back into its older identity, Attorney General Guste summed up what it would mean for the citizens of Louisiana. The decision was a "landmark," he said, that "will result in many millions of dollars of additional income to the state." Just as important, it would allow the state to preserve the ecology of the region's water bottoms without having "to buy rights or obtain permission for public use of these properties" from hundreds of private landowners.[45] And finally, the decision left the state in a much better position to defend its title to the new land against Dow Chemical Company.

Still not quite ready to give up the fight, however, the defendants sought yet another rehearing of the case. The "multiple-factor test," wrote Wilkinson, "is not authorized or approved by any law or court decision or any text book on physical geography, geology, or other scientific publication." It was instead, Wilkinson continued, "a figment of Dr. Charles R. Kolb's imagination—Plaintiffs' so-called expert." It was, of course, no more a figment than Steinmayer's, or anyone else's view for that matter. But what really annoyed Wilkinson was the court's decision to include "historical designation" as a valid classifying standard. Wilkinson put his point of view thus: "What's in a name? Paradise, Arizona, is as hot as hell in the summertime, and Hell's Hole in Nevada freezes over in the wintertime! The law does not attach any importance to a name which misnames the object to which it is applied." Even the U.S. Supreme Court, he claimed, "stated that the names applied to water bodies do not determine their character." As Wilkinson concluded, "because some old-time native or past historian attached the name of 'lake' to the water body here involved does not make it a lake when it possesses all the characteristics of a stream."[46]

Of course, an old-timer, even one who happened to be a historian, was as able to invest the waterscape with meaning as Reinhard August Steinmayer. Perhaps even more able. Whether someone like Wilkinson or his colleagues chose to credit how these people named the waterscape is another matter. The tendency to trust in science, to somehow imagine that a man like Steinmayer possessed of a lifetime of technical knowledge and experience could settle a simple factual dilemma—is it a lake or not?—is tantalizing. It is also a misplaced faith. For over a decade, Steinmayer had cornered the market in lakes and streams; his definitions, adopted by the courts, ruled. Now his monopoly on the subject had come to an end. It was not so much Kolb who triumphed here, as Wilkinson suggested. The victors, if such can be spoken of, were a far more disparate lot. They were countless mapmakers, surveyors, and others, their names obscure, who had somehow come to imagine this body of water as a lake and inscribed it as such. The words of the French critic Tzvetan Todorov are especially apt: "To represent or to say a thing is already to bring it into existence."[47]

THERE MUST BE SOMETHING about Louisiana water that makes people curious about names. Not long before the courts started wrestling with the identity issue, the novelist Walker Percy wondered how names come to mean what they do. As he sat thinking one Louisiana summer, sometime in the 1950s, Percy recalled a well-known scene from Helen Keller's life, the one in which Miss Sullivan puts Helen's hand under a waterspout, spelling the word *water* in her other hand. That was the day Helen Keller learned that names have meaning. If only one knew what really went on that day with Helen Keller, thought Percy, one could perhaps discover the key to language. Clearly something important had taken place. The word *water* was no mere sign; it was now, to Helen at least, a symbol, a word that denoted the substance called water.[48]

Louisiana is a big place, and who knows if Percy ever met his neighbors there—Wilkinson, Steinmayer, or anyone else involved in the Six Mile Lake debate. But if he had, Percy might have pointed out that naming is not a straightforward process. Naming, as Percy would have it, consists of a pairing, of the apposition of name and object, of symbolizing entity and symbolized. But it is the essence of that pairing, the relationship between the name and the object it represents, that Percy wondered about. "The symbol," he wrote, "has the peculiar property of containing within itself *in alio esse*, in another mode of existence, that which is symbolized."[49] When a body of water is called a lake and has for many years been known as such, that meaning tends to harden, to develop a rhetorical force all its own, and a powerful one at that. It would not be easy to call it something else, even if it was just for the purposes of legal classification (a common strategy in the briefs). The symbolic world knows no such boundaries.[50]

"The notion of giving something a *name*," Susanne Langer has written, "is the vastest generative idea that ever was conceived."[51] To name something is a way of comprehending it. But naming is more than simply a way of knowing. It is also an act of appropriation and control. And it is this aspect of the naming process that is central to law and property relations. To be sure, the nineteenth-century surveyors and cartographers who trudged through the Atchafalaya basin did so in search of knowledge about this obscure land. That, however, was not their only task. They were also on a mission of conquest, whether they admitted it or not. By the twentieth century, as a result of their work and that of others, that very same waterscape was a vast expanse of names, of such and such a lake, bayou, stream, and so forth. Could one sink an oil well in the midst of a nameless waterscape? Not under the strictures imposed by the economic culture of capitalism. To name is to know, but it is also to own.

Classifying and naming are part of what might be called the symbolic technology of property law. They fall into the same category as other symbolic acts that we use to declare our ownership over nature—surveying and marking boundaries, writing and registering deeds, and so forth. Names are used to order and mark nature so it can be owned. Of course, the interesting thing about names—something the participants in the legal cases learned in the end—is that their history can be extraordinarily important. Call something a lake long enough, let that meaning dominate, and it builds up a reality as real and authentic as the physical entity that rests out there on the ground, whatever it might look like at any given time.

Any name will do in the act of appropriation. But it is how well something, such as a body of water, is named that counts as far as property rights and the law are concerned. Names impose order on a disorderly natural world, but that world is so fluid and chaotic that it often defies classification. No name, no matter how accurate, precise, or well chosen, will succeed in totally capturing and appropriating a physical reality 100 percent. Ownership over the earth is thus not as straightforward or commonsensical as one might think. Whatever the power of the law, in all its impeccable logic, it was unable to contain the contradictions that emerged in bayou country where nature (and the Corps of Engineers) pushed ownership to its limit. Let the area in question look like a lake and the law fancied it a stream; encounter a stream and the law says it is a lake. So much for logic and intuition.

"We order the world according to categories that we take for granted simply because they are given," writes the historian Robert Darnton. "We classify a Pekinese and a Great Dane together as dogs without hesitating, even though the Pekinese might seem to have more in common with a cat and the Great Dane with a pony. If we stopped to reflect on definitions of 'dogness' or on the other categories for sorting out life, we could never get on with the business of living."[52] But think for a moment about the category of "lakeness," as we have, and see just how much *living* is dominated by the business of *owning*. Something to think about on a stroll around a lake.

3

Notes from Underground:
The Private Life of Water

Water taken in moderation cannot hurt anybody.
—MARK TWAIN (1866)

Perhaps you remember the Underground Man, that miserable wretch, so bitter, lonely, and worried about his liver. The protagonist of Dostoevsky's famous novel *Notes from Underground*, the Underground Man is a retired civil servant, a minor one, who lives in a filthy room just outside of Petersburg. He is so bored that all he can do is write. So he tells us about his walks on the Nevsky Prospect, his friends, and a trip to a bordello. But the weight of all these encounters with the people of the real world is too much for the Underground Man to bear. He retreats. He escapes back to his own private underground world where he can suffer his thoughts in peace.

The Underground Man never made it to Arizona, but that should not keep us from wondering what he would have thought about the people who lived there and how they treated the down-below. Indeed, with the aid of this fictional curmudgeon, we can better understand what it means to own property in a desert.

In the 1860s, while Dostoevsky was sitting in Russia

writing his novel, halfway across the world, the state of Arizona came into being. It was, by all accounts, an inauspicious place for a state—in the middle of a desert. The entire southwestern extreme of Arizona (where most of the state's population lives today) is part of the Sonoran Desert, over one hundred thousand square miles of the hottest land on earth, stretching south all the way to Mexico's Culiacán River. It is one of the most unforgiving environments in all the world. Nothing that lives survives easily here under the desert sun. This is a land of vast silences, a place of dust and heat and little rain. Phoenix averages less than eight inches of precipitation a year, about a third of Dostoevsky's Petersburg. Venture into Arizona country and you will see reminders of how hard life with little water can be: a dust storm, dark and fearsome, bearing down on a trembling little town; a decomposing burro, its stinking carcass laid out on a shriveled stretch of grass; a water hole baked so dry by the sun that the earth below it has been pried open into a furious maze of cracks and fissures.

But beneath this aching piece of earth there is hope. Under the scorched land lay an altogether different world, an underground as rich in water as the surface is poor. The water was laid down during the ice ages and rested there undisturbed for thousands of years. Then by about 1920, Arizonans abandoned the surface and turned their attention underground, mining the fossil water below at a pace that turned frantic after the Second World War. Over four hundred thousand acres of newly cultivated land came into existence in the six years following 1946. And almost none of it would have been there if it were not for the underground and its hidden water wealth. The water turned southern Arizona into a sea of green, a garden paradise that spread out into the desert like a huge oasis.

[*83*]

Beginning as early as 1940 and accelerating after the Second World War came a wave of settlers, thousands of people flocking to Arizona, to the desert itself. They came to speculate in land, to farm cotton, to chase after the American dream. Or they came simply to escape the cold and damp and retire under a brighter, warmer sky. In the decade of the forties, the population of Phoenix shot up over 60 percent to more than one hundred thousand people. And for a place that was supposed to be so hot and sparse, the desert did not look too bad at all. There were long, neat rows of citrus trees, oranges and grapefruits basking in the desert sun. There were fields and fields of lettuce, alfalfa, grapes, cantaloupe, wheat, and sweet corn, and, most prominent of all, there was cotton, growing six feet tall in places, a blanket of white that stretched out toward the horizon. One essential fact accounted for the boom, and Arizonans were standing right on top of it.

Where there is money to be made by controlling nature, it is a safe bet that there will be conflicts over property and ownership. When all those people came pouring into Arizona, headed straight for places with names such as Sunset Cove and Paradise Valley, many bought their property assuming they owned it exclusively—soil, rock, and, above all else, water. But water, unfortunately, flows. And with all those people madly pumping from the underground, sinking more and more wells, digging deeper and deeper, it soon became clear that some people were pumping water at the expense of their neighbors down the road. In the midst of the biggest boom in the state's short history, there were skeptics left scratching their heads, wondering just how private their private property was. Who really owned the underground in Arizona?

IN DOSTOEVSKY'S TIME, Arizonans were scarcely even aware of the down-under. In 1864, while the Russian was busy creating his novel, lawmakers sat down to hammer out Arizona's territorial constitution, a document that has nothing at all to say about matters underground. When lawmakers drew up the constitution, they made a list of the kinds of water to be found in the state. On that list were lakes, ponds, and streams, all of which were vested in the public and subject to the doctrine of prior appropriation.[1] That meant that every last drop of water in the state *except* the water that oozed through the ground would exist as a public reserve, giving a priority right to the first person to exploit it. There is a Latin expression that sums up this doctrine: *Qui prior est tempore potior est jure.* Put simply: First in time is first in right. Among westerners, the rule was as popular as water was scarce, which is to say that it had wide appeal, sending Arizonans on a reckless tear through the land digging canals and building dams to bring surface water to their crops.

So in the beginning, Arizona's lawmakers paid no attention to percolating water simply because almost all the water they found was on the surface. In the Salt River Valley, what would become the heart of the state's agriculture, surface irrigation began as early as 1867 when Texas Ranger Jack Swilling helped to start an irrigation company. Following his success, other irrigation ditches were dug throughout the valley, crisscrossing it with canals—the San Francisco (1871), Utah (1877), Grand (1878), Mesa (1879), Arizona (1883), Consolidated (1892)—and creating enough water to sustain over one hundred thousand acres by early in the twentieth century.[2] But the greatest boon to irrigation agriculture came in 1902 when Congress passed the National

Reclamation Act. The act made money available from the sale of western lands to reclaim the desert. Arizonans were able to use the act to convince the federal government to build a dam in the Salt River Valley, in what was one of the earliest efforts at federal reclamation.[3]

The keystone of the Salt River Valley project was over three hundred thousand cubic yards of cement standing almost three hundred feet high, measuring one thousand feet across, and named in honor of Theodore Roosevelt. When Roosevelt Dam was finished in 1911, it was the highest dam in the world. Behind it lay Roosevelt Lake, with a capacity of almost one and a half million acre-feet, enough water to flood over a million football fields to a depth of one foot. (An acre-foot is equal to 326,000 gallons.) And Roosevelt Dam was just the beginning. It was followed by Mormon Flat Dam finished in 1925, Horse Mesa Dam in 1927, and Stewart Mountain Dam in 1930. The dams turned the Salt River into a string of reservoirs for irrigating land and producing electric power, a system so masterful and efficient that it has overflowed only once since its completion.

Meanwhile, the attention of Arizonans began to wander away from the surface as the underground began to nudge its way into consciousness. Irrigation water newly brought into the valley raised the water table, causing the land to flood in places. So wells were drilled to drain the land. By 1923, the Salt River Valley had ninety-nine such extraction wells in operation. What began as a nuisance ended in bonanza as Arizonans became more and more desperate to siphon off the liquid gold underfoot.

Who was this knocking at the Underground Man's door? A swarm of farmers, speculators, and scientists come to rationalize the unseen, to observe, measure, control, and transform it into the twentieth century's greatest testament to the domination and control of nature, to make it into a *resource*. "Man is preeminently a creative animal," says the Underground Man, "predestined to strive consciously toward a goal, and to engage in engineering; that is, eternally and incessantly, to build new roads, *wherever they may lead*."[4] In Arizona, all roads headed down.

To see how the underground came bursting into consciousness, understand that beginning in the mid-1930s many farmers were interested in growing short-staple cotton as the nation emerged from the depression and cotton prices increased. Short-staple cotton, which was averaging a little over eight cents a pound in 1938, reached thirty-three cents in 1946 and then climbed as high as forty cents in 1950: an increase of 500 percent in just twelve years. Of course, it takes water to grow cotton, twice what it takes for grapes and about five times as much as lettuce. There was no way that the available surface waters of Arizona could have supported the state's cotton boom, with acreage for short-staple cotton by 1951 over two and a half times what it was twelve years before. By 1951, there were over half a million acres planted in the crop.[5] Imagine Rhode Island. Then think of what it would look like covered over two-thirds in white.

But more than just cotton was driving Arizonans underground. The decade following 1942 was one of the driest in Arizona's history. When the state land commissioner, O. C. Williams, toured the state in 1946, he could hardly believe what he saw. In Pinal County, dust was piled up so high on the road that he could see the marks made by the undercarriages of cars that had passed through.[6] Four years later, Arizona averaged just seven and a half inches of precipitation for the year, the lowest amount in the state's history.[7] In 1951, Vic Watson posed for a photographer from *Life* magazine, thrusting his arm up to the elbow in a huge crack that had opened in what had once been a water hole on his ranch south of the Grand Canyon.[8] Now it was nothing but a fractured piece of earth. Farther south, Horseshoe Lake near Phoenix, with a capacity of almost one hundred forty thousand acre-feet of water, had been drawn down so low that it almost ceased to exist.

This is where the underground came in. Faced with the drought and desiring to grow more and more cotton, Arizonans headed straight down. Vast amounts of water lay beneath the land, although no one could say exactly how much. Government scientists had begun in the 1930s to explore the underground more thoroughly. And starting in 1939, the U.S. Geological Survey began taking an inventory of the state's groundwater resources, reporting carefully on the water level as it began to drop lower and lower. By the forties, the underground was being mapped out and studied, scrutinized into so many acre-feet of water, rapidly being rationalized and forced to yield before an upward-sloping curve of economic growth. The underground would never be the same again.

No matter how much water existed down below, it was of no use unless farmers were able to bring it up from the depths. This they were able to do with electric-powered pumps. All the dams that had gone up along the region's rivers delivered water for agriculture. But the same dams also produced hydroelectric power, causing the price of electricity to fall. That was important because anyone who has carried a pail of water up a hill knows just how heavy water is. It took a lot of power to haul up water from hundreds of feet down below. With the pumps humming away, the numbers were on the march. In Maricopa County, host to the Salt River Valley, almost a million acre-feet of underground water (more than three hundred billion gallons)

WATSON AND "WATER HOLE"

were pumped in 1940. Ten years later, that number had nearly doubled.[9]

All these forces—drought, the rise in cotton prices, the fall in electric rates—converged with considerable force just south of Phoenix in Pinal County. When George Smith—professor, hydrologist, and author of Arizona's first state water code—journeyed to Pinal County's Eloy district in 1907, he found just three ranches huddled together near a small stream, struggling to fend off the encroaching desert. A few years later the drilling began. By 1930, there were still only about twelve wells of major proportion in operation. When Smith revisited the area later in the decade, forty-four new wells had been drilled, almost all of them reaching four hundred to six hundred feet below the surface. Yet in Smith's considered opinion, plenty of evidence already existed to show that the groundwater supply was overtaxed. According to Smith, pumping in 1936 was almost twice what it should have been to assure an adequate future supply. But the farmers kept on drilling. In the fall of 1939 and through that winter, over thirty new wells were drilled in the Eloy basin alone.[10]

One of the people Smith ran into in Eloy was John Goree. Some years later, Goree recalled their conversation. He was about to drill some new wells when Smith advised him not to. "You are wasting your time, young man," Goree remembered Smith saying. "There is no water here. There are too many wells here now. They are going to pump it dry."[11] But Goree did not listen, and neither did his neighbors. What Smith observed in the late thirties was just the beginning, the opening act of the biggest underground water crusade in Arizona history. In 1940, Pinal County farmers were pumping well over three hundred thousand acre-feet of water. By the end of the decade, they were using almost three times as much. The water table was getting lower and lower, and by 1950, farmers had to reach forty-two feet deeper into the ground to strike water than they did ten years before.[12] The water level sunk and so did the ground on top of it, causing long cracks to ripple across the desert.

With the land caving in, it is perhaps a good time to return to the Underground Man. "Man likes to create and build roads," he says, "that is beyond dispute. But why does he also have such a passionate love for destruction and chaos?"[13]

SUPPOSE FOR A MOMENT that at the close of the Second World War, you and your family, like thousands of others, had packed your bags and journeyed to Arizona to buy a piece of the desert, a nice little place to grow cotton or retire from the world. Did purchasing the land give you title to the down-below, to the soil, clay, rock, and, above all, the water beneath your dream home?

That was a question many Arizonans wrestled with following the war. As farmers and others in the state used their pumps to plunge ever deeper into the ground, they created "cones of depression," pockets in the aquifer that sloped downward in the direction of the wells. Dig a well large and deep enough and you will find those cones growing bigger, sucking water directly out from shallower wells nearby, precisely as happened in parts of southern Arizona.

Thus many people in the state might rightly have wondered whether they had a legal right to the water under their land, because if they did, then those with the deeper wells had no business taking it. But until 1945, Arizona law had very little to say about the underground. The territorial constitution made no mention of percolating water, and neither did a state water code written by George Smith and passed in 1919. The 1919 code made water in definite underground channels subject to prior appropriation, but water percolating through cracks and holes in the earth escaped unnoticed.[14]

The result was strikingly undemocratic: in Arizona all water was not created equal. By failing to mention percolating water, Smith helped create a legal fiction. Under the law there were two kinds of water: one contained by definite boundaries (a lake or stream, even an underground one), and another that dribbled freely, unrestrained through the ground. Knowingly or in blissful ignorance, Smith took Arizona down a path quite at odds with what would be the prevailing wisdom of his field. In the twentieth century it was learned that surface and percolating water were indeed connected to one another, that (in the words of George Smith himself some years later) they were both "one water."[15] But in Arizona the law was the law, and what it said, even as late as the 1950s and beyond, was that there were two different kinds of water and each would be treated differently. All water except for the percolating kind was subject to prior appropriation; the rest was governed by the so-called common law rule. There was nothing at all common about the rule, despite its name. It was a rule founded on private property that considered percolating water to be part of the soil and therefore the property of the overlying landowner, so long as it remained under his land.

There were rumblings in the 1940s calling for an underground water code that would have changed all this, but it was not until the Bureau of Reclamation stepped into the picture that serious discussion got under way. In 1945, the bureau announced that it had no intention of carrying out its plans for piping Colorado River water into southern Arizona—what became the Central Arizona Project—unless the state passed an underground water code, replacing the rule of absolute ownership with some kind of state control. Unwilling to let the Central Arizona Project slip away—if only because it had fueled the greatest land boom in Arizona history—the legislature was moved to action. The new code required the registration of irrigation wells but otherwise did nothing to stem the rapid depletion of the underground.[16]

So the pumping continued, and so did the efforts to pass another groundwater code. There was a proposal to make all groundwater public property and give the state land commissioner authority to regulate the appropriation of water. When that bill did not pass, there was a proposal to shift to a correlative rights rule, which would allocate scarce water based on the quantity of land owned. When that did not work, another bill transformed all water not already being used into public property and restricted how it could be employed. And when that too failed, there was yet another bill, legislation designed (like all the rest) in one way or another to loosen the grip that private property had on the underground.[17] Finally, in 1948, the state passed a new underground water code.[18] It set up critical groundwater districts, allowing the state land commissioner to stop additional drilling in such areas. But the law was merely a stopgap measure, a gloss on the 1945 code; it did nothing to weaken the passion for owning and mining the underground. In the five years after the act passed, the amount of water pumped out of the underground increased almost 50 percent. The increase alone totaled a huge one and a half million acre-feet of water—more than the entire capacity of Roosevelt Lake.

It was the older, more established farmers who were the driving force behind the water codes. They were the people most threatened by the land speculators and other newcomers who swarmed to the state after the Second World War to pump the desert dry. Of course, the older water users were also pumping as hard as they could to increase their own personal fortunes. But they had been at it longer and felt entitled to priority over the new "pump and run" boys. In truth, there were probably few people in the state opposed in principle to private property. Yet to those in favor of changing the law, the problem was that private property in percolating water simply was not private enough. They wanted a groundwater code that would replace the common law rule of absolute ownership with one that afforded some regulation of the underground; they were counting on such a rule to favor the longtime users over the newcomers.

Of course, many found the fine points of the law beside the point. "We bought our land with the idea that we owned it," said Henry McKeen, a farmer from Wilcox, by which he meant that he owned the water and everything else that happened to rest under his property. McKeen, speaking in 1952, noted that when the government transferred land to homesteaders, they deeded it by the acre. Nobody said anything about volume, not a word to the effect that one "owned the land six feet deep or ten feet deep or one inch."[19] To McKeen, the silence meant that landowners in Arizona owned the underground and its water, period. "I sure don't understand much law," said rancher Cecil Miller in 1948, "but I understand we have been operating on the theory that the water underground belonged to us."[20]

The same culture that after the Second World War was busy erecting chain-link fences and planting shrubs to divide one plot from another was also desperate to own the underground and its most precious resource, no matter what. Just how desperate? Cecil Miller learned about one of the proposed laws to regulate the underground, to get rid of private ownership of percolating water and, as he put it, say that it belonged to everybody "share and share alike." And this was his reaction: "It reminds me of passing a law saying we are going to fine you ten bucks for every time you kissed your wife in the last ten years. You will break a bunch of us."[21] It was an apt analogy; they loved their families, but they loved their property too.

Casey Abbott, who farmed over twenty-five hundred acres of land in the Salt River Valley, had a similar fondness for private property. In 1947, when a bill to shift to a system of correlative rights was before the legislature, he drove to the state capitol in Phoenix. Abbott, age sixty-one, had lived in Arizona for close to twenty-five years. He had seen the amount of irrigated land in the state almost double in that time. And when he stood before the committee considering the bill, he made it very clear that he liked the law as it was. The state had done well for itself with private ownership of the underground, Abbott pointed out. He believed the pending bill was "class" legislation, calculated to benefit the big irrigation districts while "we fellows outside are through." "I saw the last three years of the gun game," Abbott said, referring to the demise of the gunfighting era in the late nineteenth century, "and in all that rough life I never saw an evil thing like this."[22]

Neither had S. E. Jordon. Jordon had yet to sink a well on his land, and now he believed he might never be able to. "I have 160 acres," he said. "I have spent my life there. Now, who in the Sam Hill wants to tell me what to do and how to do it."[23]

There was no telling just how far one might go in the name of private property. Armon Cheatham went farther than most, all the way to Arizona's supreme court. In 1919, Cheatham and his wife sold their dairy in Duncan, Arizona, packed up their wagons and Model T Ford, and trekked half-way across the state. They headed for Laveen, a small dusty town on the southern edge of Phoenix. At first they ran a general store, but before long they had saved enough money to buy a house and forty acres of land. Over the years the Cheathams amassed a sizable amount of property. By the early fifties they were growing cotton and feed for their dairy herd on roughly two thousand acres, almost half of which they owned.[24]

The trouble began in the late forties when Cheatham's neighbor, Tom Bristor, found his well running dry. Bristor left Ohio in 1922 and went to Arizona for relief from sinus trouble. He was trading one kind of headache for another. In 1929, Bristor bought a twenty-four-acre ranch in Sunset Cove near Laveen. A year later, he drilled a well that was one hundred seventy feet deep to give him water for cooking, washing, and other household needs. Then in 1945, the water level in the well began to drop. Down, down, down went the water until four years later he was pumping up nothing but air and some rust flakes. It cost Bristor twelve hundred dollars to drill a new well to a depth of two hundred thirty feet.[25] Down the road, Lester Jennings and his wife found that their well had also run dry. And that was John Roberts's story and George Shelton's. The same thing happened to Claude Melick and William Porter and Parley Oram, thirty-eight people in all, with precisely the same story to tell.

It was not hard to figure out where the water had gone. Between 1946 and 1948, Armon Cheatham (an ironic surname as it turned out) sunk four new wells, averaging roughly four hundred feet deep, giving him a total of eleven. One of those wells pumped thirty-five hundred gallons of water per minute. The water was then shipped almost two miles to land that Cheatham leased. Seeing all this, Bristor and his dried-up neighbors hired a lawyer and took the Cheathams to court.

The case that resulted is among the more famous in the history of Arizona water law. *Bristor* v. *Cheatham* began in Maricopa County Superior Court. Cheatham's excessive pumping had cost Bristor and his neighbors a great deal. There was the money they spent to bring fresh water into their homes when the wells went dry. There was the expense of sinking new wells. And then there was the money it cost them on paper as the market value of their property plummeted when the water ran out. Collectively, they estimated their losses at over two hundred thousand dollars, and the lawsuit was designed to get that money back. The suit also sought an injunction that would put an end to Cheatham's pumping.

They rested their case on the following argument.[26] Cheatham, they believed, had been making an unreasonable use of the water. He was not only pumping an excessive amount of water with his powerful pumps; he was also—and this is what really galled Bristor and his neighbors—using the water to reclaim desert land miles away from his property. It was one thing to pump water and use it on the land where it had been pumped. It was quite another thing, the plaintiffs claimed, to pump off water to irrigate crops somewhere out in the desert.

To this the Cheathams responded, it is our land, we own it, and we will do whatever we like with the water that is under it. No law said that they could not pump the water off to more distant lands. Indeed, the Cheathams argued, the law said precisely what they had claimed, that percolating water was private property, theirs to own and use however they wished. On this score, the case law did seem to support the Cheathams, although the issues were not nearly as clear-cut as their lawyers made them out to be. For example, an important case from 1904 sanctioned the distinction between percolating water, which was subject to private ownership, and all other water.[27] In another case from 1931, percolating water was held to be "the property of the owner of the land, subject to the rules of the common law."[28] According to the opinion, since the legislature had never specifically stated that prior appropriation ruled in the case of percolating water, the *expressio unius* maxim applied (expressing one thing excludes another), which is to say that it fell under the common law rule of absolute ownership. The opinion implied that percolating water belonged to the overlying landowner, although it made no definite conclusion about exactly what rule should govern.[29] On all this the Cheathams got no argument from the Hon. Thomas J. Croaff, who dismissed the complaint made by Bristor and his neighbors.

Bristor and company then appealed to the supreme court late in 1949. It took the court two years to make up its mind on the matter. In that time, another half million acre-feet of water disappeared from down below. The surge in pumping resulted mainly from a steep rise in cotton prices; short-staple cotton soared from twenty-eight cents in 1949 to over forty-one cents the following year. Meanwhile, the amount of acreage devoted to the crop more than doubled between 1950 and 1951; by 1952, half the cultivated land in the state was planted in cotton, close to seven hundred thousand acres in all. Into the ground they went, irrigation farmers all driving their wells deeper and deeper to deliver up whatever hydraulic wealth the earth had left to offer. Severe drought further intensified the pumping (1950, recall, was the driest year in the state's history). While the court was off deliberating, the water table in one part of Maricopa County alone dropped an average of more than nine feet.

It took the supreme court just a few pages to put a halt to this underground stampede. When the court finally ruled on the case, some compared the decision's impact to an atomic explosion that rocked the down-below like never before (an image that must have resonated powerfully in the wake of Hiroshima, especially in the American Southwest where the destructive force of the bomb was first unleashed). On January 12, 1952, the court decided that percolating water was no longer private property. Just the day before, Arizona landowners had gone to sleep thinking they owned their land to the center of the earth. When they woke up the next day, the earth was cut out from under them.

Judge Marlin Phelps sized up the situation for the court. He reasoned that if the rule of private ownership stood, it would lead to "the inevitable exhaustion of all underground waters." So in a remarkable move, Phelps overturned all prior legal precedent and ruled that percolating water was subject to prior appropriation just like all the rest of the water in the state. "The common-law rule that water is inherent in the soil and belongs to the owner of the soil . . . is itself an anomaly," Phelps wrote. The crux of the matter was really quite simple: There just was no way to own something as fluid as water. To support his argument, Phelps dug out a law review article by Marion Rice Kirkwood, dean of Stanford University's law school for more than two decades. Private ownership of percolating water "is quite unrealistic," Phelps quoted the article as saying. "It rests on the notion that the overlying-land owner has possession of all that is below the surface of his land, and that there is no distinction in this respect between rock and water. But in fact there is a difference: rocks stay in place, water moves."[30]

"Rocks stay, water moves" was an old argument that went back at least as far as the eighteenth century when the jurist William Blackstone made a similar remark. (Water, he wrote, "is a moveable, wandering thing, and must of necessity continue common by the law of nature; so that I can only have a temporary, transient, usufructary property therein.")[31] Clearly water is harder to own exclusively than solid rock. But such an understanding, seemingly so commonplace, had not stopped Arizona's courts from ruling that percolating water could be privately owned. Nor had such a realization stood in the way of Cecil Miller, Casey Abbott, or any of the thousands of people who seemed to think that they owned their land clear to the earth's molten core.

Private property in the underground was real all right. At least there were a lot of people in Arizona who believed in it. Consider Fred Ironside. He was a believer, a man who swore that farmers in Arizona owned the water below their land just like they owned their homes. A lawyer who led the fight against the *Bristor* decision, Ironside had close ties to the farmers of Pinal County, which was sinking because of all the water that had been mined out of the ground. Those farmers too were believers. Even before the *Bristor* decision, they were out in force opposing the enactment of an underground water code. Hundreds of them packed into an auditorium to hear Ironside speak. "Under the proposed code," Ironside told them, "the water will be taken from you."[32] That was all those farmers needed to hear; they banded together in the Farmers Defense Association.[33] Let the decision in *Bristor* stand, they reasoned, and it would turn the entire state back into desert. "If this situation continues," one Pinal County farmer said, "we'll all be out of business. We'll all be broke."[34] Rumors spread that banks were going to cut off loans to farmers. Orders for farm equipment plummeted. An economic Armageddon was rippling across the state, all because three supreme court justices had decided that private property was not so private after all.

Then the court had second thoughts. One of the people unhappy with the supreme court's decision was Judge Arthur La Prade. La Prade dissented from the majority decision in *Bristor*. He believed that the issue in the case was far narrower than the majority had thought. The court was not being asked to decide on private property in percolating water. All it needed to determine was whether Cheatham had made a reasonable use of the water by pumping it to land a few miles away from his property. That was a persuasive argument, compelling enough to convince Judge Rawghlie Stanford (who had sided with the majority in January) to change his mind. On February 26, 1952, the court granted a rehearing. For some forty restless nights after the first ruling in *Bristor*, farmers worried about the underground. But when the court granted the rehearing, it nullified the earlier decision and foreshadowed the return of the underground to its former owners.

And that was precisely what happened when the court reversed itself the following year. "Under both the civil and common law," the new decision reads, "ground water belonged to the owner of the soil."[35] The only wrinkle in this endorsement of absolute ownership was the court's statement that percolating water must be used reasonably. Whether Cheatham had acted in a reasonable way in shipping water off to reclaim the desert was a question that the court said still must be decided. Since Bristor and his neighbors did not go forward with the lawsuit, we can never know how the Arizona Supreme Court would have answered that question. But we can be certain of this much: private property in the underground ruled again.

About the only thing Tom Bristor got out of his four-year struggle with Armon Cheatham was his picture in *Business Week*. There he sat sipping coffee in his kitchen, looking gaunt and depressed, a set of gauges on the wall behind him measuring the water pressure in his well. It was more than the other plaintiffs in the case had to show. Of course, Bristor and his neighbors still owned the underground. But with the Cheathams pumping away, there was hardly anything down there worth owning anymore.

If private property in percolating water was so unrealistic, as Arizona's highest court had briefly held, then why was it so real to Bristor? One can surely argue, as many have, that the notion of private property in percolating water is an illusory one. It is hard to imagine exclusive ownership over something so elusive, there one minute and gone the next, headed off toward wherever gravity might take it. Private property in underground water, so the argument goes, is a massive act of denial. And yet the illusion persisted. Thousands of people in Arizona all fooled themselves into thinking that they possessed the unpossessable. It was as if an army of confidence men had descended on the underground.

If it was not possible to own the underground exclusively, it certainly was possible to *think* one owned it in such a way. Such a thought, illusion or not, had important consequences. For in truth, private property in the underground was hardly private after all; there was no denying the social and environmental interdependencies that tied together people and water in the desert. How convenient to imagine

that one owned the underground and its water and not have
to deal with the grim social reality that resulted from such
a notion. It was as if a pair of dark glasses across one's eyes
could hide the ecological impact, the wells running dry, the
people unable to afford the stronger and stronger pumps that
it took to reach ever deeper into the ground. Percolating
water in Arizona had come to exist as an abstraction, severed from other kinds of water, seemingly cut off from the
world of power relations where some and not others benefited from the control of nature.

There is not nearly as much privacy in private property
as one might think. A fence has yet to be invented that
could completely shut out the world of social and environmental relations. But in Arizona enough walls had been
built around underground water to convince more than a few
people that what they did on their land was entirely their
own business.

COMES NOW, the Underground Man. What can an alien-
ated Russian civil servant, a fictional one no less, possibly
have to tell us about water and property in a desert thousands of miles away? More than one might at first suspect,
but we have to listen carefully. Out there in the desert is
his voice: "Man likes to create and build roads, that is beyond dispute. . . . But . . . may it not be that . . . he is
instinctively afraid of attaining his goal and completing the
edifice he is constructing? How do you know, perhaps he
only likes that edifice from a distance, and not at all at close
range, perhaps he only likes to build it and does not want
to live in it."[36]

It happens that when the Underground Man spoke those
words he had in mind London's Crystal Palace. Close to fifteen hundred tons of iron, glass, and geometric calculation

spread out on a commanding spot on Sydenham Hill, the palace was originally built in 1851 for the Great International Exhibition. For the Underground Man, the palace symbolized, so many have said, all that was wrong with modern life. In its iron and glass, its mathematical precision, the Underground Man saw a building radiating such exactitude that it threatened an end to all creativity and dreaming, a building that cast a shadow so long, dark, and fearsome that no one would dare speak out against it. The Underground Man is just dying to thumb his nose at the palace and all that it suggested about modern life, the rank materialism, rationalism, and alienation. But he cannot. So hard it is to question the palace, to point a finger at modernity's impeccable logic. Building is one thing, the Underground Man knows full well, but living in what we have built is something else again.

And yet the Underground Man, the critic Marshall Berman has pointed out, is more of a modern man than one might think. For one thing, he accepts engineering. According to Berman, the Underground Man has no quarrel with building new buildings or with any of the other engineered aspects of modern life. What the Underground Man worries about is what happens when engineering is sapped of its creative potential and descends into mere calculation and materialism. "The activity of engineering," Berman writes, "so long as it remains an activity, can bring man's creativity to its highest pitch; but as soon as the builder stops building, *and entrenches himself in the things he has made*, the creative energies are frozen, and the palace becomes a tomb."[37] It is perhaps no accident that the Underground Man lives a squalid life largely devoid of things, that he is clearly a man of little property.

Who knows exactly how the Underground Man felt about

property. But the point about building roads can be applied as readily to the underground in Arizona as it can to the futuristic Crystal Palace in nineteenth-century London. We moderns are always building, building at times simply for the sake of building, with little or no thought of where we are going or what life will be like once we get there. Let the building stop for a minute, put away the drilling rigs and pumps, and a kind of emptiness echoes out across the desert, all the wells, all the people holed up on their land, fenced in and owning to the center of the earth.

Question: Does the landowner own the water, or is it the other way around? In the dreams dried up into dust piled alongside Tom Bristor's old well, in the various broken spirits walled up inside their property lines, lies an answer to this question. Such is the thrill of owning.

4

Cloudbusting in
Fulton County

*Do you know the balancings of the clouds, the wondrous works
of him who is perfect in knowledge?*
—BOOK OF JOB 37:16

On the afternoon of Saturday, August 22, 1964, David
Fulk achieved an unusual distinction. At half past one, with
the sky a blend of clouds and sun, Fulk rumbled into Big
Cove Tannery, Fulton County, Pennsylvania, in a pickup
truck with big round fenders and curves all over. A generator for vaporizing silver iodide stood upright in the back.
When he stepped out of the truck, Fulk, age twenty-five,
became the first person in American history to be arrested
for trying to change the weather.

David Fulk played a small role in one of the boldest
schemes ever dreamed up for dominating nature. The will
to control the weather stretches deep into the American
past.[1] But weather modification, in its modern incarnation,
dates from only 1946 when Vincent Schaefer of General
Electric, a self-trained chemist and high school dropout,
produced snow artificially in an ordinary home freezer.
Schaefer discovered that something as simple as dry ice
could make some clouds precipitate. Later that year, Schaefer flew east over the Hudson River in search of a cloud to

test his discovery. At fourteen thousand feet, he found one and seeded it with dry ice, causing snow to fall. "This is history," exclaimed Schaefer's colleague Irving Langmuir—himself a Nobel laureate in chemistry—as he rushed forth to greet him when he landed.[2]

This was history all right, but *cultural* history as much as any other kind. Weather modification had its roots in the most American of preoccupations: the success story. Without advanced educational degrees, without even a high school diploma, Vincent Schaefer, who worked his way up at GE from his start as a machinist, had discovered a new technology with the potential to change the world forever. Weather modification was the control of nature made easy—technology for the people. What Schaefer had done looked so simple, it seemed anyone could do it. Consider the story of an Arizona rancher who after reading about Schaefer's discovery in *Life* magazine, took off in a plane of his own to seed clouds over his drought-stricken property. And he succeeded, not just in making snow but in making history: He too was written up in *Life*.[3] Weather modification had stunning cultural resonance. It was a technology that everyone could support; after all, as the saying goes, everybody talks about the weather, and now, finally, somebody was doing something about it.

Schaefer's discovery was far too important to be left only in the hands of GE and the occasional rancher. Before long the military embarked on weather modification research with the hope of adding it to its cold war arsenal. Nor did the prospect of weather control escape the eager eyes of American business. Everything in America had a price tag, and now even the weather seemed to be entering into the realm of markets and commodities as weather companies—fifteen in all by 1965—sprang up to capitalize on the bold

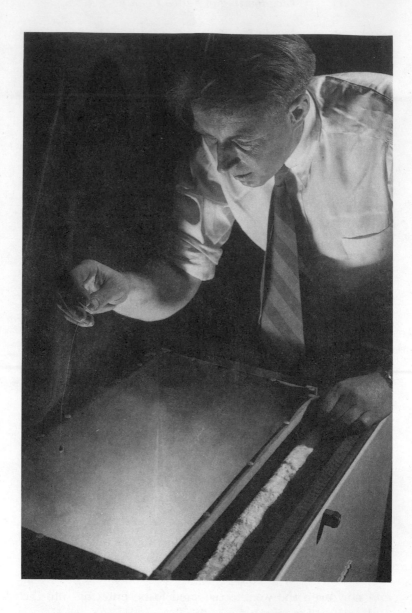

SCHAEFER MAKING HISTORY

new technology. The scope of that technology was wide indeed. It promised rain and snow on command, as well as an end to lightning, fog, and hail. By 1952, it was estimated that cloud seeding was taking place over almost three hundred million acres of land, an area almost three times the size of California.[4]

It had long been said that rain falls on the just and unjust, the rich and the poor alike. But weather modification threatened to destroy that truism. No longer would all humanity be equal before the forces of nature. Weather modification offered science, the state, and business a chance to appropriate nature in the most literal way, to control sun and rain and clouds however they wished. It only remained to be seen who the winners and losers would be in this grandest of plans to dominate the natural world. This is the story of what happened when weather modification came to south central Pennsylvania.

FULTON COUNTY. A near-perfect parallelogram of close to three hundred thousand acres nestled in the Appalachian Mountains. In 1960, about two thousand people lived there, most of them spread out across the valley that plunged through the center of the county. The landscape unfolded in rectangles of corn, wheat, hay, some peaches, and the occasional strawberry patch, dotted in barn red, splashed with whitewash, and thick with the sounds and smells of cattle, hogs, and chickens. Like much of rural America in the second half of the twentieth century, Fulton County had seen better days. There were nine hundred farms in the county in 1960, and what poor ones they were. The average value of land and buildings per farm was just over seventy-five hundred dollars, the lowest reported figure for all of the sixty-seven counties in Pennsylvania.[5] Fulton County was poor, dirt poor.

It was also dry. A drought descended over the region beginning in 1962 and lasted for the next five years, driving farmers further into debt as their crops shriveled. The drought made weather history, affecting not just Fulton County but the entire Northeast and beyond from Maine as far south as Virginia.[6] In Fulton County, there was a lot to talk about: the streams that dried up into dust, the crop yields that tumbled, the livestock that went hungry, and the schools that closed for lack of water as the earth was baked dry as a bone. The summers of 1964 and 1965 were by far the worst ones. In the words of one farmer, there was scarcely enough rain in the latter summer "to wet your shirt."

As farmers watched the sky dry up, as they hauled water to their livestock, kicking up dust as they went, they began to wonder if the dry weather was truly an act of God. For what distinguished this drought from all the others, what made it stand out from the average drought, if such ever existed, was not its severity, duration, or the hardship it caused but one simple fact: some Fulton County farmers believed this drought was man-made. And the man they thought had made it was Wallace Howell.

Wallace Egbert Howell was born in 1914 in Central Valley, New York. Early on in his career, he worked as a meteorologist for Mid-Continent Airlines and then served in the military. He went to school at Harvard and MIT and wrote a dissertation entitled "Growth of Cloud Drops in Uniformly Lifted Air." He forecasted at the U.S. Weather Bureau. He directed the Harvard–Mount Washington Icing Research Project. He consulted to the U.S. government on weather modification. Finally, he went into the weather business. The founder and president of W. E. Howell Associates, a private company specializing in weather modification, Howell had by the 1960s worked on over sixty weather-related projects, from New York to the Philippines and elsewhere in between.[7] What he sought to do in his business was something that others had done countless times before, transform nature into a commodity. With airplanes, chemicals, radar, and whatever else he could muster, Howell worked to control the weather, to extend his mastery such that he could sell it and make a profit.

There was no way the farmers of Fulton County, struggling to endure the drought, could afford to pay for Howell's service, however much it might have helped. It took money to hire Howell, and the people who had it suffered the least from the dry weather. Howell was invited to Pennsylvania by the Blue Ridge Weather Modification Association, a group made up of commercial fruit growers in neighboring Franklin County and in other nearby areas, including parts of Maryland, Virginia, and West Virginia. They were able to survive the drought by relying on irrigated water. However, there was one thing about the weather they did want to change: they yearned for an end to the hailstorms that pounded the region. The group had organized in the wake of a fierce storm that rolled through the area in the summer of 1956, a deluge of hail so severe that it destroyed the fruit and stripped the bark off trees. Not long after, the Blue Ridge association hired the Weather Modification Company of San Jose, California, to cloud-seed in order to chase the hail away.[8]

The hailstorms continued. On June 29, 1960, as an evening thunderstorm swept through the area, hailstones, some the size of baseballs, fell on Franklin County—contiguous to Fulton—defoliating trees, shattering windows, and smashing roofs. A severer storm pummeled Franklin County two years later. Winds gusted up to thirty-eight miles per hour as the storm hit on July 23, 1962, destroying peaches and apples in more than three-quarters of the county's commercial orchards.[9]

The following spring Wallace Howell arrived in the area and went to work on the weather. His tools included two single-engine planes—a North American T28 and an AT6—and one hundred ten ground-based generators. Silver iodide was the key ingredient. The planes were flown through thunder clouds streaming silver iodide out the back; the generators vaporized the chemical, which was then carried up into the clouds. Once in the sky, the silver iodide helped to increase the number of hailstones to the point where there were so many that not enough supercooled water remained for any of the stones to grow large enough to threaten the fruit crop. Or so the theory went. For two consecutive summers starting in 1963, Howell's company activated its generators and flew boldly through thunderheads to ward off hail in a targeted area that included Franklin County, Pennsylvania, and parts of Maryland, Virginia, and West Virginia. But it is extraordinarily unclear what effect, if any, Howell and his company had on the weather. And in any event, by 1965, Howell and his equipment were gone.

He did not leave voluntarily. Howell was forced out by a rising tide opposed to weather modification. As early as 1962, farmers in Fulton and Franklin counties became suspicious that weather modification had contributed to the drought that blanketed the region. That same year, vandals chopped down over one hundred young plum trees at the Heisey Orchards, which was a member of the Blue Ridge Weather Modification Association. And rumors surfaced

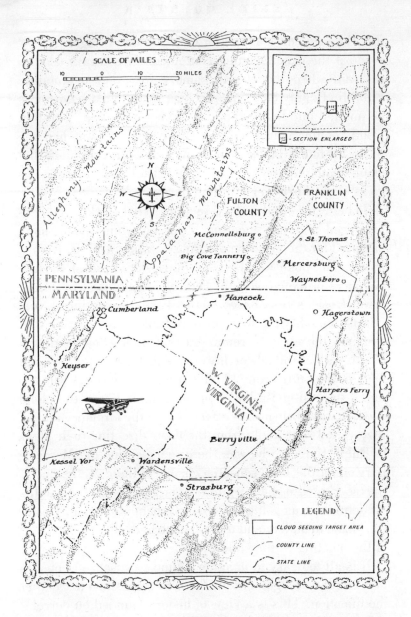

CLOUD SEEDING TARGET AREA

that the company's supply of irrigated water might be poisoned if the cloud seeding continued. "We always used to get rain when the clouds came across that mountain," Franklin County dairy farmer Jack Beck told a reporter as he pointed into the distance. "But not any more, with that cloud seeding going on. I've stood here and watched the plane fly into a black cloud, and within five minutes that cloud scattered and the sun shone. I tell you, somebody's going to get hurt over it unless they stop."[10]

To help sort out the cloud seeding issue, Beck and others organized a public meeting. Over four hundred farmers gathered for the event on a spring evening in 1962. Among those who spoke was Charles L. Hosler, head of the department of meteorology at Pennsylvania State University. It was Hosler's view, based on twenty years experience, that efforts to modify the weather were futile. "You may as well spit into the air," he remarked that night, "as seed rain clouds with chemicals or any other substance. . . . You just can't push nature around." Meanwhile, the farmers who endured the two-and-a-half-hour meeting believed the cloud seeding was having some effect. "Take the airplanes away," they yelled repeatedly from the floor, directing their pleas to Ralph Heisey, who was there representing the Mercersburg orchard.[11] They sensed a change in their weather since the cloud seeding had begun, and no scientist, whatever his credentials, was going to convince them otherwise. Hosler was made to understand this when he had to be escorted out of the meeting by the state police.

It is all too easy to imagine a simple causal relationship between the drought and the farmers' opposition to weather modification. This is a view of history founded on correlations, a vision of the past that lines up events neatly in rows, drawing arrows from one to the other. Such an understanding of history is useful at times but is not without its risks. Chief among these is that the past will emerge as a mere caricature. For in truth, the opposition to weather modification was not simply a product of the drought. That is not to say that the drought did not matter but only that dry weather alone hardly accounted for all the opposition to cloud seeding.

Weather modification was scarcely a neutral technology and, drought or not, it was going to have important social consequences. Cloud seeding would benefit some and not others, and in this case it threatened to breach the bounds of the shared "weather culture" of rural Pennsylvania. The weather is not simply some objective force; different cultures make sense of the weather in their own special ways.[12] Fulton County's weather culture was founded on equality before the forces of nature, where every person stood in the same relationship to the weather as every other. The weather was a vast leveling force that paid no attention to wealth, character, class, or the kind of car one drove. The farmers of Fulton County knew their weather. They had seen enough storms and sat through enough dry summers to know that just a few inches less rain could make a big difference in their lives. But they also knew that their suffering, however long and hard, was the work of nature; it was the hand that they had been dealt. And then there came weather modification. Marl Garlock, a Fulton County farmer, put it this way: "From the beginning of time until recently, the weather has been controlled by Our Creator. Why then should we have men professing to control our weather today, to suit the whims of a few people, with so many left to suffer so much."[13]

Weather modification did more than threaten Fulton County with drought. It shook the entire moral economy of the weather to its very core. And in the summer of 1964, over four hundred farmers gathered in Fulton County to do something about it. Together they formed the Pennsylvania Natural Weather Association (PNWA), an organization dedicated to one, and only one, kind of weather. They elected local newspaperman Guy Oakman to be their chairman. The editor of the *Fulton Democrat*, Oakman believed weather modification to be among the worst abuses ever heaped on the region's farmers. He saw through the veneer of hope and opportunity that Howell said weather modification offered the region's people, farmer and orchardist alike. And when he stripped away all the false promises, what Oakman discovered in cloud seeding was a technology with the power to benefit some at the expense of others. "We fail to see," he wrote, "how any one group should and does have the right to attempt to control the weather at the expense of another and larger group of people."[14] Some things are better left to nature, to chance, to God or some other higher force, and the weather, according to Oakman and his supporters in the PNWA, was one of them. As Delmar Mellott, a farmer and PNWA member remarked, "Those who talk of the practice of weather control in any way should take note to Psalms 46:10: 'Be still and know that I am God.' "[15]

According to Oakman and the PNWA, their right to natural weather was founded on one of the most cherished institutions in American history, private property. "We fail to see how anyone, with a just regard for the rights of a property owner," wrote Oakman, "can ever hope to apply the science of weather modification without infringing on these inherent rights."[16] Landowners, whether wealthy commercial fruit growers with a thousand acres each or poor dairy farmers with just a hundred or so, owned not just their land but also the air and weather above it, believed Oakman and the PNWA. It was not then simply a question of whether cloud seeding contributed to the drought. "We believe the question is much broader and more basic," wrote Oakman. "We believe the question is: Does a man have the right to have the weather above and around him remain in its natural condition and undisturbed? We believe he does."[17]

This same concern with natural weather prompted the townships of Fulton County in June 1964 to pass a series of ordinances. The one for Ayr Township stipulated that "no person or persons shall install, construct, erect, operate, or maintain any equipment, machinery, or device within the said township designed to, or intending to, or which has a tendency to install, eliminate, regulate, or interfere with the normal rainfall or precipitation." It was this law that David Fulk ran afoul of that Saturday in 1964. Fulk had been sent into Fulton County ostensibly to operate a ground-based generator. But he was really sent there because Wallace Howell wanted to test the legality of the Ayr ordinance outlawing weather modification. So Fulk was taken into custody and brought before Justice of the Peace Lewis Strait, who found him guilty as charged. That result was hardly surprising. There was, after all, an affidavit signed by Harvey Richards, the officer on the scene, swearing that Fulk operated the generator. There was the ordinance stating that operating a generator was contrary to town law. And then there was Strait's own opinion of weather modification. Strait seemed to prefer his weather the natural way, precisely as God would have it. His advice to his drought-stricken neighbors, given in a letter to the local newspaper, could not have been clearer:

> Will it rain?
> Why does it not rain?

Read the Bible:—
I Kings 8:35–36.
II Chronicles 7:13–14.
Amos 4:7–11.

L. W. Strait, J.P.[18]

Before David Fulk left for his home in West Virginia that Saturday, he posted a bond in the amount of two hundred eighteen dollars. The money signaled Fulk's intention—actually that of Howell and the Blue Ridge organization—to appeal the decision against him. Meanwhile, Oakman and the PNWA hired a lawyer and decided to bring a case of their own. "These people are not a bunch of wild eyed farmers going about with torches, conducting a witch hunt," said Clifford Weisel, the PNWA's new legal counsel. "They are farmers with a lifetime of work and accumulation being threatened by the actions of a group who appear to have no consideration for their neighbor."[19] So on January 8, 1965, Weisel and the PNWA decided to do something about their inconsiderate neighbors. They filed a lawsuit in the Fulton County Court of Common Pleas against the Blue Ridge Weather Modification Association and Wallace E. Howell himself.

WALLACE HOWELL had run into trouble with the law before. Sometime around 1950, the city of New York, suffering from a water shortage, hired Howell to seed clouds in the Catskills, the source of the city's water supply. The trouble began when the Nevele Country Club, located in upstate New York, sued the city. The owners of the club argued that Howell's cloud seeding threatened them with floods and damaged their business by scaring off sun-loving vacationers. Refusing to grant Nevele the injunction that it sought, the New York Supreme Court found that the interests of the city and its millions of people far outweighed any damage the club might endure. In passing, the court noted that Nevele clearly had "no vested property rights in the clouds or the moisture therein."[20]

There was a lesson to be learned in the New York case, a lesson not lost on Wallace Howell. The opinion is brief, a mere five paragraphs; it cites no case law, and for a very good reason: there was none. So long as the weather remained beyond human control, there was no one to sue and no opportunity for law to be set down. Suddenly, with the advent of weather modification, the common law was forced to confront the dilemmas raised by a new technology that promised the control of nature on a scale never before imaginable. The potential for litigation was vast, even frightening, as Howell himself realized. Where would judges turn for advice when landowners sued because they believed someone had stolen their weather?

Though there was no case law, the common law was not completely silent on the matter. The seventeenth-century jurist Lord Edward Coke had written *Cujus est solum ejus est usque ad coelum*,[21] meaning, He who owns the soil owns upward to the sky.[22] Such an understanding would seem to have offered landowners a solid basis on which to sue a cloud seeder who ventured over their land. The problem was that apart from Lord Coke and a handful of long-dead jurists, nobody really took the ad coelum doctrine seriously, especially by the twentieth century.[23] The doctrine, based as it was on an unbounded concept of ownership, would not survive when faced with an economic order in need of a more dynamic set of property rights to spur efficiency and growth. With the beginning of modern air travel, what little credibility the doctrine once had was now firmly thrust aside. One opinion written in 1936 put it bluntly: The ad coelum doctrine "is not the law, and . . . never was the law."[24]

If Lord Coke could no longer be taken at his word, that still left the question of how the law would settle disputes over clouds and weather. One idea was to employ an analogy from some other area of property law.[25] There were lots of possibilities to choose from, for after all, this was hardly the first time that the law had tried to wrap the language of property around the natural world. For example, there was the law pertaining to wild animals, the law of oil and gas, the law of surface and percolating water—all cases in which property rights to nature had to be decided, however elusive the resource might seem. Surely one of these resources was comparable to weather and clouds. Quite a few pages—none of them conclusive—were written by legal scholars on which area of law offered the best analogy to the weather. But in the end, a bird was not a cloud; nor was oil, gas, or percolating water exactly the right analogy for the weather.

With so many directions for the law of property to move, so many jurisdictional issues, there was but one sensible place to look for help, the federal government. In 1951, the year after the decision in the New York City case, Howell made a pitch for federal control over weather modification.[26] Nobody, or at least nobody with the power to do something, seems to have heard him. The task of regulating conflicts over the weather fell into the hands of state and local governments, where it would continue to rest, despite Howell's objections. There was a lot to object to, in part because when Howell took to the skies over the Blue Ridge area, he passed over no fewer than three states, and each would have its say about the weather. By early 1965, the legislatures of

Maryland, West Virginia, and Pennsylvania, all under pressure from natural weather groups like the PNWA, had cloud seeding legislation before them. A West Virginia bill banned all commercial cloud seeding. A Maryland bill declared a two-year moratorium on all cloud seeding—commercial or not—until the controversy over hail suppression could be sorted out. And Pennsylvania, after an earlier bill failed, introduced a proposal similar to the one in West Virginia.[27] A war was being waged against cloud seeding, and the Blue Ridge Weather Modification Association did about the only sensible thing it could do: retreat. In March 1965, the association relieved Howell of his duties.

That caused Howell to think seriously about his less than warm welcome in the Blue Ridge area. In his view, there was one main explanation for the opposition. Very simply, the farmers in the region had held him accountable—quite mistakenly he believed—for the dry spell. The opposition to his cloud seeding activities fluctuated with the weather. The hotter and drier the weather, the more intemperate became the forces opposed to cloud seeding. But that opposition was nothing that a little rain could not fix, and when things cooled off, according to Howell, the objections disappeared. This simple causal relationship went way back to the start of cloud seeding in the Blue Ridge area. In 1957, when the cloud seeding began, a severe drought caused farmers to protest. That opposition was washed away by the adequate rains that fell over the next four growing seasons. Then drought returned again in 1962, and so did the objections to cloud seeding. It all could be captured in just one short equation: opposition was inversely proportional to rainfall. That cloud seeding had caused the drought, as many farmers presumed, was nothing short of preposterous to Howell. It was not possible for him or anyone else to stop the rain. "If it was," said Howell, "Robert Moses would have hired us for the World's Fair."[28]

Howell was so fixed on the skies over the Blue Ridge area that he failed to see that this was a clash not of clouds but of cultures. One culture took the weather however it came, and the other did not; one subordinated itself before the weather, and the other aspired to dominance; one liked to think the weather affected everyone equally, and the other was eager to change that; one was willing to let fate and God and whatever else intervene, and the other sought to liberate itself from nature, transforming the weather into a simple commodity that could be bought and sold like a million other things in America. It was these two cultures, these two vastly different ways of making sense of the weather, that stood staring each other in the eye.

But Howell did not see it this way. To his mind, what had gone wrong in the Blue Ridge area was in part a technical problem. In his words, "The situation in which large numbers of people can be persuaded that it is scientifically possible, and actually the current practice to break up rain clouds and suppress rainfall, is one that exhibits a failure of communication between the scientific community and a considerable segment of society."[29] What had gone wrong in the Blue Ridge area had nothing at all to do with morality, culture, or anything else; the problem there was purely technical, a mere "failure of communication." That, according to Howell, was easy enough to fix: simply have meteorologists talk more with the public. Understanding was everything.

There is no doubting what it was that Howell wanted the public to understand. "It has been a truism of weather modification," he wrote at one point, "that it concerns every citizen whose life is affected by the weather, and that means all of us." In Howell's view, everyone had a stake in weather modification. With just a little education, any reasonably enlightened citizen could be made to realize its true value, to see the enormous potential benefits of mastering the elements. The control of nature was not simply a technical task or a scientific charge. It was a civic duty. To be sure, as Howell put it, "the channels of scientific communication cannot hope, of course, to reach every crank who holds peculiar notions."[30] But as for the rest, they would surely see that support for weather modification was part of what it meant to be a good weather citizen.

It might be a while before Howell's message dribbled down to the ordinary American, months and years at least, time that Howell and his colleagues in the field of commercial cloud seeding really did not have. Control over the sky was slowly slipping away from them as state governments in the Blue Ridge area moved to restrict weather modification. So again Howell cried out for federal intervention. This time he took that message directly to the U.S. Congress. In early 1966, Congress had legislation before it seeking to shift authority for weather modification away from the National Science Foundation to the Department of Commerce. "There is nothing tentative in my mind about the present need for Federal preemption of the power to regulate," Howell told a Senate committee. "A power vacuum exists that is being partially filled by inconsistent State and local legislation, in some instances capricious and ill-advised."[31]

Nor was Howell the only one who called out for federal intervention. He was joined by a lawyer named Edward Morris, who had successfully defended a California utility company against a charge of more than ten million dollars in damages from floods caused by its cloud seeding. Something along the lines of the Atomic Energy Commission or the Federal Communications Commission, Morris believed, needed to be set up, and fast. "This Federal agency might eventually plan weather by zones or by days, sell or buy weather to or from other agencies, possibly even make decisions as to the 'best' weather for certain times and places."[32] Morris was dead serious.

Meanwhile, in Pennsylvania, a bill prohibiting all commercial cloud seeding for two years passed the legislature and just missed becoming law when Gov. William Scranton—explaining that he did not want to stand in the way of scientific progress—intervened in July 1965 to veto it. Then in November, act 331 became the law. It said that if a county passed a resolution saying that weather modification adversely affected the region's welfare, then all cloud seeding would be banned there. By February 1966, both Fulton and Franklin counties had such resolutions on the books. The so-called cranks had gotten the upper hand.[33]

It was all so easy to make those opposed to weather modification into cranks and crackpots, so tempting to see them for what, in this view, they were: dirt farmers with toothless smiles, tobacco juice drooling down their faces, so wretched and deprived that they were unable to see what was in their own best interests. If the natural weather people could not be educated, at least they could be diagnosed. Some years later, in the seventies, Richard Heisey, whose family owned the Mercersburg orchard where workers once carried guns to protect themselves, reflected on those opposed to the cloud seeding: "Ninety percent of the people who were up in arms were, caliber-wise, mentally, ah . . . Well, let me tell you, there are people in this area who think that when man landed on the moon it was fake. They think it was filmed in the desert."[34]

WHEN THE FULTON COUNTY cloud seeding trial opened on February 2, 1966, David Fulk did not make it to court. The weather stopped him. A blizzard, one of the worst in recent years, kept him away. The snowstorm, as far as anyone knew, was natural weather, exactly the kind of weather the PNWA had come to court to fight for that day.

The PNWA and its lawyer, Clifford Weisel, arrived at the courthouse in McConnellsburg prepared to argue their case for an injunction against the cloud seeding. They had one main story to tell and it went like this: Back in the old days, certainly as far back as anyone now alive could remember, thunder clouds would roll up over Fulton County and rain would pour down on the land. The weather came and went, but of one thing farmers could be certain: when those clouds approached, dark and forbidding, there would be rain. Things began to change in 1963. Those same clouds swelled out over the sky, and just as they looked about to burst forth with rain, a plane would appear, and the cloud would be gone, the weather changing to bright sunshine beating down on the dry land. If landowners had a right to the natural weather over their land, argued the PNWA, then Wallace Howell and the Blue Ridge association had interfered with this right, and it stood to reason that the court should stop them from any further cloud seeding. It had been agreed beforehand that the PNWA's lawsuit and the appeal of Fulk's arrest brought by Howell and the Blue Ridge association would be combined into one trial. Finally Fulton County farmers would learn who really owned the weather.

Boyd Hawkins was the PNWA's first witness.[35] He was fifty-seven and had lived in Fulton County since 1917. All told, he farmed about five hundred acres of land, where he grew corn, hay, barley, oats, wheat, and potatoes and tended to a variety of beef cattle. About the weather over this property, he had nothing unusual to report until 1963 or so. From that point on, he could recall at least a dozen instances similar to this one:

I was sure we were going to get a good rain, clouds come up in the west, and several occasions, I would hurry in to close the barn doors or cover up the hay I had in the field and sometimes before I would get the door closed, I would see a plane or hear it come into these clouds, two or three times, and as a result, before I would get to the house, the color had changed, and the cloud had broken up and scattered and it got light, and it got so towards the last if I heard or saw the plane before I closed the barn doors, I wouldn't bother.

Lewis Gordon, a farmer from Big Cove Tannery, told a similar story. One day in the summer of 1964, Gordon went to the Fulton County Fair. To escape the afternoon heat, he took cover under a wagon. Lying there looking up, he saw a storm start to blow in from the west, when all of a sudden a plane appeared and "in a few minutes, the cloud just broke up in small parts and went north and south, and that was it." William Lucas was getting ready to cut hay when the same thing happened in June 1964. And that was Delmar Mellott's story, too. A farmer and manager of a farm supply store, Mellott traveled a good deal around the area and said wherever he went farmers were talking about the weather and those airplanes. Something odd had been going on in the skies over Fulton County.

To Robert Frantz, lawyer for Howell and the Blue Ridge association, fell the task of cross-examining these witnesses. His strategy was clear. He wanted to get them to admit at least the possibility that weather modification could benefit them. He did not have a whole lot of success.

"Would you object if your farm got more water as a result of cloud seeding?" he asked Boyd Hawkins. "I object to the cloud seeding," Hawkins replied. "I will take my dry weather and my wet weather as it comes." And that was essentially William Lucas's answer and Delmar Mellott's, too. As Mellott put it, "I feel that if there has to be talking to a—what I call the rain maker— . . . I would rather do it on my knees, not on the telephone."

Frantz questioned witness after witness. Not one gave an inch—until he reached Jack Beck, the last person the PNWA called to the stand. If any witness would budge it would be Beck. He had been involved in the cloud seeding dispute since at least 1962 when he helped organize a public meeting on the issue. At the very least he was open-minded. Once he had even agreed to meet Wallace Howell to talk the matter over. But by the time the trial came around, Beck was dead set against weather modification. A member of the PNWA, Beck felt that nature ought to take its course, "just the same as we took this big snowstorm," he said, referring to the blizzard that had kept Fulk from coming to court. As he had done all along, Frantz tried to draw Beck into admitting that if cloud seeding caused more rain to fall, then surely he would not quibble. But Beck made it perfectly clear that he could never embrace weather modification. "I do not feel I can do that and still treat our neighbors the same." Frantz would not give up. What if the scientific community accepted weather modification, Frantz replied, what if it definitely worked, then surely you would favor it. No, apparently not even then. "Can we all make hay the same day?" Beck answered. But the point was lost on Frantz, completely lost.

Luckily for Frantz, he did not have to change the minds of the natural weather people. He only had to convince one man about weather modification: Judge W. C. Sheely. Frantz put Howell on the stand and had him explain that during the period in 1964 when he was cloud seeding, one study showed an increase of 14 percent in the area's precipitation. Rarely do statistics tell the whole story, and in this case the figure was a dubious one, there being an almost one in four likelihood that the increase was due to chance.

Of course, there was no way that anyone could say exactly what had gone on in the sky over Fulton County and thus no way to know if Howell had influenced the weather. But Frantz was determined to convince Judge Sheely that whatever went on up there, Wallace Howell was no irresponsible opportunist out to make a fast buck. He had Howell review his credentials for the court: service for the military, the Weather Bureau, the Blue Hill Observatory of Harvard University, consultant to the federal government, editor of a major journal, right down to the exam he took to become a certified consulting meteorologist, which he passed, of course. One could call Howell a lot of things, but unqualified was not one of them. And Howell had F. W. Reichelderfer, chief of the U.S. Weather Bureau for almost twenty-five years, to back him up. Called to testify as an impartial witness, one whose appearance both sides in the case agreed to, Reichelderfer described Howell as "one of the most responsible of those who are experimenting and operating in the cloud seeding field."

That was not all Reichelderfer had to say. Although admitting that commercial weather modification was a controversial area, he explained that cloud seeding had not caused the drought in Fulton County. The drought, which encompassed an area many times the size of Fulton County, came from a change in atmospheric circulation. Moreover, he had a way to account for all those eyewitness reports of clouds breaking up, one that had absolutely no connection with airplanes, silver iodide, or Wallace Howell. It had to do with something called the "lee effect." Fulton County lay on the lee side of the Allegheny Mountains. When a wind blowing from the west encountered a mountain, it was forced up, temporarily compressing and cooling the air, perhaps condensing enough moisture for a cloud to form. Then as the air reached the other side of the mountain—the lee side— it had room again to expand; the air would heat and the cloud might disappear. All this, according to Reichelderfer, could happen in just fifteen or twenty minutes. There was nothing unusual about it. Insofar as Reichelderfer could be trusted—and who would dare not trust a man of his stature—Fulton County farmers had been getting natural weather after all.

But just in case Sheely chose not to believe him, Frantz had filed a number of briefs to steer the judge toward his clients' position. The PNWA had argued from the start that landowners had a right to the natural weather over their land. *Natural* was the key word, and Frantz took it upon himself to explain to the court what this word meant to a culture that during the postwar period had grown so obsessed with the technological domination of nature. What was the meaning of *natural* in a world so eager to master the environment, whatever the cost? What could possibly be natural in such a world? Or as the law might phrase it, what were the natural rights to which a landowner was entitled?

To this last question, the common law had proffered an answer. When someone bought a piece of land, the common law extended a bundle of so-called natural rights. These included riparian rights and the right to "lateral and subjacent support," which prevented someone from digging a hole around one's property that might compromise the land's integrity. They included the right to air that was reasonably free from pollution, the right to natural drainage, the right to use the land for any legitimate purpose, to build on it, farm it, and so forth.[36] It was indeed a long list, and it seemed fair, even natural, to think that the weather in its undisturbed form ought to be a part of it, or so the PNWA and its lawyer argued.

The word *natural* comes of course from *nature*, which is one of the most complicated words in the English language.[37] And *natural* too is a very slippery word. To Frantz and the cloud seeders, it did not mean undisturbed or pristine. For such a strict interpretation would just about put Howell and anyone else interested in controlling the weather out of business. There would be lawsuits galore as landowners found their rights to the peaceable enjoyment of their land invaded. Frantz made it clear that we must search elsewhere for the true meaning of the word. "The so-called 'natural' rights theory expounded in the legal periodicals," Frantz wrote, "does not in fact mean natural to the extent that it is absolutely undisturbed by any other activity." "A more correct interpretation of the theory," he explained, "would be that if a landowner were to receive a 'normal' amount of rain, he would have no grounds for complaint."[38] Here was the true meaning of *natural*, and it was so simple and obvious it is a wonder that no one had thought of it before. The word when used in the sense of a "natural right" to the weather meant above all one thing: normal.

So what was normal weather? As Frantz saw it, normal weather changed a great deal. "Fluctuation," he explained, "is a normal property of the weather with which every person must of necessity contend. Favorable weather brings enormous economic benefits, unfavorable weather enormous loss." In the capitalist language of costs and benefits, there were only two kinds of weather that mattered: weather that favored economic growth, and weather that did not. Nor was there any question as to which kind of weather the cloud seeders were promoting. But to sell Judge Sheely on capitalist weather, Frantz had to make it seem as natural as any other weather that the world had known. In other words, the weather fluctuates, it has always done so, and what would it matter if it proved a bit more changeable, especially if it did so for the sake of extra profit? "Fluctuations of the weather," wrote Frantz, "whether natural or artificial, intentional or inadvertent, are not per se unexpected or improper as long as weather modifying acts do not cause the atmosphere to deviate beyond its normal range of fluctuation."[39]

If the weather did not change, if the wind blew always from the west, if the sun stayed out each and every day, there would hardly be anything to talk about. The fact that it did change, however, gave Frantz a whole lot to say. And what he wanted to say the loudest was this: weather fluctuations are normal, natural, even if they resulted from human contrivance. Weather modification, as Frantz would have it, was part of the natural order of things, just one more change that people should expect to endure. Of course, he left unsaid that cloud seeding served some interests and not others, that the drive to master nature, to chase hail from the skies, was supposed to benefit the fruit growers who hired Howell, not the farmers who lived nearby.

Those sweltering farmers, padding back and forth over grass so dry it crunched underfoot, would have to wait more than two full years for a ruling on the cloud seeding. Meanwhile, Judge Sheely died. He was replaced by Judge John MacPhail who read over the testimony, listened to oral arguments, and finally on February 28, 1968, wrote two opinions. MacPhail affirmed Lewis Strait's lower court decision against Fulk for violating the town ordinance against cloud seeding. The town, MacPhail believed, had every right to enact such legislation and Fulk was guilty of violating it. But far more was at stake in *Pennsylvania Natural Weather Association* v. *Blue Ridge Weather Modification Association*: MacPhail would decide if landowners had a right to the natural weather over their land.

Not much had been said by jurists on the question of natural weather. There was, of course, the New York case involving the Nevele Country Club, in which the court ruled that one could have no vested right in a cloud. But MacPhail was certain that the statement was dictum—an opinion offered in passing—and in any event no legal authority supported it. MacPhail also mentioned a group of Texas cloud seeding cases, but none of them ruled on ownership rights in the weather. MacPhail was on his own with this one. He reasoned that it would make a mockery of the entire idea of property if a landowner were not entitled to some reasonable expectation of natural weather. After all, what farmer would buy a piece of land after eyeing the local weather, only to find that his neighbor had some scheme to alter the rain pattern? Moreover, MacPhail believed a precedent existed which gave landowners a right to the airspace over their land. The 1933 Pennsylvania Aeronautical Code said a landowner had title to the air above to the extent that it was "necessary to the enjoyment of the use of the surface . . . subject to the right of passage or flight of aircraft." What all this added up to, in MacPhail's view, was "that every landowner has a property right in the clouds and the water in them." But that right was not an "unqualified" one. He felt that weather modification done by the government to benefit the public, as opposed to private interests, must be permitted.[40]

"Men are not God," MacPhail quoted a Catholic priest as saying, "and they do not succeed well when they attempt to play God." That said, MacPhail could not find any evidence that Fulton County's farmers had suffered from what Howell had done. Nor, for that matter, did the drought coincide with Howell's presence in the area; it had begun before he arrived and continued after he had left. And finally, MacPhail had one last reason for dismissing the PNWA's suit. In the time it took for a decision to be reached, the state legislature had passed a law that regulated cloud seeding by setting up a weather modification board. Disgruntled farmers, or anyone else who found their weather tampered with, could now—thankfully, no doubt, from the court's perspective—turn to the board for relief.[41]

That MacPhail had said landowners had a property right in the clouds, that he had thrown his support behind natural weather (albeit subject to government intervention)—all this did not count for very much among Fulton County's farmers. Property is founded on possession, and as yet there was still no way to own the weather, to define and fence its boundaries as one would a field or pasture, even a burned-out one. There was, in the end, no way really to own the weather, at least not in the sense that one owned land or a house.

Still, that did not stop the natural weather farmers from arguing, in effect, that they had absolute dominion over their property. Back before the nineteenth century, that argument held a good deal of weight. But a world where everyone had an absolute right to landed property, where no one could use their land without worrying about what effect it might have on their neighbor, was a world where economic development could scarcely proceed. So it came to be that landowners' rights to absolute and peaceable enjoyment of their property were sacrificed to benefit economic growth. Once landholders had, for example, a right to the natural flow of water across their property; *aqua currit et debet currere, ut currere solebat*: water flows and ought to flow as it has customarily flowed, was the saying. By the Civil War, however, a far more instrumental vision of property had come into play. No longer were landowners entitled to absolute dominion over their land and water; the natural flow rule was eclipsed by a "reasonable use" standard. Which is to say that courts would weigh the relative efficiencies— the costs and benefits—of a particular water use. Whether it was natural or not was beside the point.[42]

Now landowners in Fulton County were being forced to forsake the natural flow of water *above* their land. There was no way that weather modification could continue to be practiced if all landowners had an unqualified right to the natural, God-given weather over their property. MacPhail was saying that the relative merits of weather modification would have to be weighed against the damage to property interests. The law would favor the use that generated the greatest economic utility for society as a whole—nature and God notwithstanding. Thus was the *moral* economy of the weather in Fulton County overturned by a far more market-oriented one.

If one took weather modification and put aside its technical jargon, forgot for a moment its wildest promises, what was left in the end was the incorrigible will to dominate and control nature.[43] But it was domination that did not profess to benefit everyone equally. The German philosopher Max Horkheimer said it best: "Domination of nature involves domination of man."[44]

5

Three-D Deeds:
The Rise of Air Rights
in New York

*We will probably be judged not by the monuments
we build but by those we have destroyed.*
—NEW YORK TIMES, EDITORIAL (1963)

Singer Tower was once the tallest skyscraper in the world.
Over six hundred feet of red brick and steel lavished
with pediments, balconies, cartouches, and consoles and
capped by a huge mansard roof with decorative lantern—
this futuristic gem was completed in 1908 for the famous
sewing machine company. Its lobby resembled a cathedral,
replete with sixteen exquisite piers of Italian marble, intri-
cately detailed bronze railings, and a vaulted ceiling with
glass domes. It boasted its own little generating plant for
producing power and heat; special vacuum tubes set into
the walls to make office cleanup easy; even a network of
pipes made especially for cleaning silk hats. Not a detail
was overlooked, right down to a system for distributing ice
water—cooled in a basement refrigeration plant—to tenants. Singer Tower was truly a modern building, a structure
ahead of its time. Perhaps that is why Ernest Flagg, who
designed the tower, believed it to be "as solid and lasting
as the Pyramids."[1]

Flagg died in 1947. Two decades later, Singer Tower lay

in a steaming pile of plaster and dust—courtesy of the Lip-sett demolition company. Superintendent Harry Glick, whose crew leveled the tower, laughed when he was re-minded by some reporters that back in 1908 Singer Tower held the height record before being overshadowed the fol-lowing year by the seven-hundred-foot Metropolitan Life In-surance Tower. "History moves fast," Glick remarked. "I've been in demolition work for nearly forty years—on jobs ranging from chicken coops to skyscrapers. My father was a demolition man. He and his partner in the Louis J. Cohen Wrecking Company took down the old riding academy at Fifty-ninth Street and Fifth Avenue to make room for the Savoy-Plaza, and now *we've* taken down the Savoy-Plaza to make room for General Motors. History moves fast."[2]

An inexorable economic logic drove Lipsett's wrecking ball. For all its beauty and elegance, the tower simply did not maximize the value of the site's air rights. It contained only a little more than four hundred thousand square feet of office space at a time when buildings four or five times that size were going up. Airspace had become a valuable com-modity by the twentieth century, and only faint hearts would shy away from bulldozing the past to realize the future. No such hearts existed at U.S. Steel; the company built a fifty-four-story structure with 1.8 million square feet of office space atop Singer Tower's corpse. So eager was the company to capitalize on the new building's economic potential that it secured control over a plot of land south of the site and landscaped it into a plaza; that move earned U.S. Steel a zoning bonus that allowed the plaza's unused air rights to be transferred to the site of the imposing steel behemoth. To-day the building looks like the work of a steel company. Fin-ished in 1974, the structure amounts to a monumental ad-vertisement for its product, featuring exposed steel girders evenly stacked one on top of the other. Thus did Singer

Tower become the U.S. Steel Building, which became One Liberty Plaza when the company chose *not* to make its headquarters there. It was evidently more lucrative to stick with its current lease and rent out the new space on lower Broadway.[3] Welcome to New York.

In the modern world, Karl Marx once observed, "everything seems pregnant with its contrary."[4] Elsewhere, he explained why in a famous passage: "The bourgeoisie cannot exist without constantly revolutionising the instruments of production, and thereby the relations of production, and with them the whole relations of society. . . . Constant revolutionising of production, uninterrupted disturbance of all social conditions, everlasting uncertainty and agitation distinguish the bourgeois epoch from all earlier ones." "All that is solid," he concluded, "melts into air."[5] But what would happen when all that was left was air? Answer: It too would melt. In the modern world, there is modern property, of which airspace is the quintessential example. Cut off from the land below, airspace has little, if any, territorial allegiance. In the century after Marx's death in 1883, New York City's air was distilled into a act of exchange values. Airspace became *real* estate, the better to own and trade it.

In a culture in which everything must have an owner, even something as diffuse as airspace could become property. How did this come to pass? What did the transformation of airspace into a commodity that could be owned and traded mean for New York and those who lived there? We must search for the answers to such questions to better understand the dilemmas of modern living, to make sense of ourselves, our cities, and the world we have made—and destroyed.

FOR CENTURIES, land was a two-dimensional affair. When lawyers in Blackstone's day (1723–1780) spoke of owning real property in land, it was the earth's surface that they generally had in mind. Blackstone himself wrote that land comprehended in its "legal signification any ground, soil, or earth whatsoever; as arable, meadows, pastures, woods, moors, waters, marshes, furzes, and heath."[6] It is, of course, true that Blackstone mimicked Lord Coke's famous ad coelum maxim (he who owns the soil owns upward to the sky).[7] But nevertheless, it was the surface of the earth that concerned those in a society based primarily on agriculture. One could walk the boundaries of such real estate, spell them out in metes and bounds, revel in the neat and ordered expanse of two-dimensionality that unfolded across the countryside. Landed elite and commoners alike had both feet planted firmly on the ground.[8]

The same was largely true in America as well. Jurists like James Kent paid homage to the ad coelum maxim; but it is hard to believe, in a society based largely (through the nineteenth century at least) on the tilling of soil, that property owners thought of real estate as anything more than the earth's two-dimensional surface.[9] Certainly if possession is at the root of ownership—a commonplace in the law—it is hard to imagine that landowners really thought their "land" extended upward to the sky. As late as 1897, a treatise writer explained that "land means in law, as in the vernacular, the soil or portion of the earth's crust."[10]

But in the twentieth century, all this began to change. With the rise of modern property, land took on a much broader meaning. The leading case of *Butler* v. *Frontier Telephone Company* illustrates the point. Butler sued the company when it stretched a wire over his land in Buffalo, New York. Neither the wire nor any supporting pole touched soil owned by him. Did Butler own the airspace over his land? Was he deprived of possession of that space by the telephone company's wire? In 1906, the New York Court of Appeals found for Butler. It reasoned that "space above land is real estate the same as the land itself."[11] Possession is founded on an understanding of the earth as a discrete set of ownable *things* (a point explored in chap. 1). By equating airspace with real estate, the court established the reality of this new form of property. "This case," wrote one legal scholar, "is an unequivocal commitment to the view that the land-space above the surface is subject to possession and ownership in the same complete sense that the surface is."[12]

"Land," another legal writer observed in 1928, "has been the most corporeal of corporeal things. It is *real* estate. Can an abstract thing like space be bought and sold as land? The air as such obviously cannot."[13] But call what was above the ground air*space* and property would plunge straight into the third dimension. Transformed into a thing, into real property, airspace was severed from the terra firma, cut adrift and catapulted into the world of property and trade.

In 1927, the Chicago Union Station Company sold the air rights needed for the Daily News Building. Meanwhile, Marshall Field bought air rights from a railway company and built the huge Merchandise Mart (finished in 1930), once the largest building in the world, with more than seven miles of hallways alone.[14] With the aid of three-dimensional deeds, financiers in New York, Philadelphia, Baltimore, and Boston all began capitalizing on the air in their respective cities. "Within the memory of the youngest of us," Theodore Schmidt told the American Bar Association in 1929, "millions of dollars' worth of usable space has been reclaimed from the wastes of a generation ago, to the gain of all concerned." Thus did real estate lose its attachment to the earth and become *deterritorialized*. "Conveyancers and lawyers," Schmidt explained, "are now for almost the first time required not only to *think*, but to *speak*, of land ownership in terms of *three* dimensions."[15]

That was 1929. But by then New Yorkers had already been talking about air rights for almost thirty years. The city's first encounter with modern property began in 1903 with the decision by the New York Central Railroad to re-build Grand Central Station. Until this time, the station (first erected in 1871) and its railroad yards occupied a stretch of land north of Forty-second Street on the city's east side. The plan called for electrifying the trains and relocating the terminal complex underground on a two-level platform. An engineer named William Wilgus proposed that with the terminal located belowground, buildings could go up on the "air rights" (a term he coined) above. "The keynote in this plan," he explained, "was the utilization of air rights that hitherto were unenjoyable with steam locomotives requiring the open air. . . . Thus from the air would be taken wealth with which to finance obligatory vast changes otherwise nonproductive. Obviously it was the thing to do."[16]

Cashing in on that air first meant tearing down what existed above Forty-second Street, including about two hundred buildings. Demolition has been big business in New York ever since. With the land now cleared of its past, workers exploded one million pounds of dynamite and hauled almost three million cubic yards of rock and soil out of the earth to make way for the new terminal complex. The station alone took ten years to build. Completed in 1913, the building is a stunning Beaux Arts inspiration. The main facade on Forty-second Street features Corinthian columns and huge arched windows topped by Jules-Alexis Coutan's graceful Roman statuary. On the air rights nearby, seven new buildings were initially planned, including the Manhattan, Belmont, Vanderbilt, and Biltmore hotels.[17] The buildings were set on a steel and concrete roof that covered the tracks below; a special insulation system absorbed the vibrations caused by trains underneath. Eventually, air over some twenty-eight acres owned by the railroad was made available for similar ventures.

Building on air was a futuristic fantasy come true, but it was hardly the only product of the turn-of-the-century urban imagination. Property's new three-dimensionality also found expression in New York's 1916 zoning law, the first of its kind in the country. Prompted by the construction of the massive Equitable Life Assurance building (1915), which cut off light as far as four blocks away, the zoning law established height and setback rules. (The Equitable building is 27% smaller than the structure U.S. Steel later erected across the street to replace Singer Tower.)[18] Under the 1916 law, a tower could reach a limited height before it had to shrink to only 25 percent of the building plot. The 25 percent tower could then reach as high as one liked. Zoning, however, was more than just a form of self-protection for property; it was a vision—in three dimensions—of what the city could become.

It is useful to compare the 1916 zoning law with the other major exercise in urban dreamwork promulgated a century before: the Manhattan grid. The grid, developed by Simeon deWitt, Gouverneur Morris, and John Rutherford in 1811, divided the city into more than two thousand blocks (12 north-south streets and 155 running from east to west). The Dutch architect Rem Koolhaas called the Manhattan grid "the most courageous act of prediction in Western civilization: the land it divides, unoccupied; the population it describes, conjectural; the buildings it locates, phantoms; the

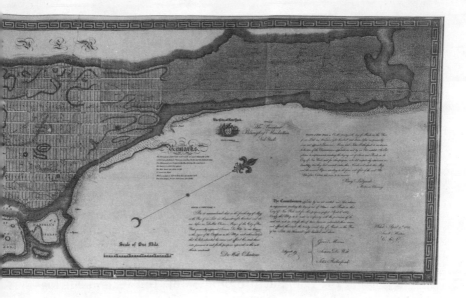

MANHATTAN GRID: COMMISSIONERS' PLAN OF 1811

activities it frames, nonexistent." Not merely an incredible prediction, it was also an amazing act of arrogance. "Through the plotting of its streets and blocks," Koolhaas continued, "it announces that the subjugation, if not obliteration, of nature is its true ambition."[19] What the grid did horizontally for the land, zoning did vertically for the sky. The 1916 law created more than two thousand imaginary boxes. It was a three-dimensional design for the city, and before long developers sought to make the most of each zoning box, maximizing profits by filling every square inch with concrete and steel.

The new geometry of modern property spurred one of the biggest building booms in Manhattan's history. Since at least the Civil War, the city's economy had been based largely on the manufacture of apparel. But manufacturing activity peaked around 1919 and was later eclipsed by a new postindustrial service economy.[20] White-collar professionals—managers, brokers, lawyers, accountants, and so on—were flooding into the city to work. What they needed, of course, was office space to conduct their business. There were just three office buildings in the Grand Central area in 1900; in 1937, there were one hundred three. During the 1920s alone, sixty-four new buildings went up with a colossal twelve and a half million square feet of rental space.[21]

Frederick Jackson Turner once declared that the American frontier had closed in 1890; New York developers proved him wrong. A huge frontier was lurking overhead—just waiting, it seemed, to be occupied. To the seven air rights ventures over the tracks leading out of Grand Central were added new hotels and office buildings. Slowly the holes over the terminal complex were filled in like a giant vertical jigsaw puzzle inching toward completion. First came three new hotels: the Marguery on Park Avenue between Forty-seventh and Forty-eighth streets (1916–1917); the Commodore on Lexington Avenue and Forty-second Street (1917–1919); and the Ambassador up on Fifty-first Street (1921). Then came six more ventures in air, including: the Park-Lexington Building (1922–1923); the Roosevelt and Park Lane hotels (1922–1924); the Graybar Building (1926–1927); and the grand, ornate New York Central Building (1927–1929), a thirty-five-story tower with two traffic tunnels carved through it which could be seen from miles around. One historian called it "a fittingly extravagant conclusion to the orgiastic decade." And finally, there was the Art Deco Waldorf-Astoria (1930–1932), which occupies the entire block between Forty-ninth and Fiftieth streets stretching from Park to Lexington, its dual towers, all six hundred-some feet of them, resting on over two hundred steel pilings. Because it stands on the air over a railroad yard, the Waldorf has a very small basement, and thus its distinguished guests must tolerate the oddity of a wine "cellar" on the fifth floor. All told, the Central and Harlem railroads in 1930 reaped four million dollars in revenue from the leasing of air rights.[22]

Where New York once produced clothing, now more and more it was becoming a huge factory for the production of space. As the philosopher Henri Lefebvre has argued, capitalism, to survive, extended its grip over "space in its entirety," not just the land but the earth below and the sky above, up and down as far as it could reach in the name of surplus value and profit. "The 'commodity world,'" he writes, ". . . which formerly encompassed only goods and things produced in space, their circulation and flow, now govern[s] space as a whole, which thus attains the autonomous (or seemingly autonomous) reality of things, of money."[23] It was this very commodity world that colonized the airspace over New York City. The modernization of air started there at the turn of the century. A new geometry transformed airspace, liberating it from the land and converting it into private property. Real estate, the most tangible, corporeal of things, seemed to be disappearing into thin air. At the same time, airspace, a three-dimensional abstraction, became a *thing* that could be owned and sold. Thus was air welcomed into the modern world; a stroll down Park Avenue was all it took to prove it.

FORTY YEARS AFTER Grand Central Station was finished—eighteen thousand tons of steel, Corinthian columns, Mercury sculpture, bronze chandeliers, and Botticino marble assembled in over ten years of construction—Robert Young, chairman of the New York Central, owner of the property, announced that he was going to demolish the building. In 1954, Young said that with its mounting debt, the railroad could no longer afford to ignore the value of its air rights. On the ashes of Grand Central, Young proposed a huge office tower that would loom higher than the Empire State Building.[24]

The building was never constructed. Instead, workers leveled a six-story office building just to the north of the station to make way for a fifty-nine-story tower, a 2.4-million-square-foot hulk of concrete and steel that at the time was the biggest office building in the history of the world. The infamous Pan Am Building (now Metlife) was built big and cheap to capitalize on rental revenue. But Pan Am is mainly remembered for blocking off the view up and down Park Avenue. That view, provided one could see it, had changed a great deal by the time the Pan Am Building was finished in 1963. Low-rise apartment and office buildings constructed earlier in the century were replaced by structures that filled the zoning box more completely. The twelve-story Montana Apartments at 375 Park Avenue became the forty-story Seagram's Building (1958). Down the block, the Marguery, also at twelve stories, became Union Carbide at fifty-two (1960). McKim, Mead, and White's 277 Park Avenue apartments, again twelve stories, became Chemical Bank at fifty (1962). It was the New York Central, of course, that mainly benefited from the remaking of the Grand Central area. The company realized higher profits from leasing more air rights.

Grand Central Terminal itself was spared, but only briefly. In 1967, the demand for Manhattan office space swelled. The city was on the brink of another building boom. Of the two hundred new office buildings that went up on the island between 1953 and 1973, 40 percent alone appeared after 1966. In other words, office space totaling seventy-one million square feet was built between 1967 and 1973.[25] Imagine the Empire State Building. Now imagine fifty more of them. In 1967, the New York Central sought to take advantage of the demand for midtown office space by proposing a tower to sit directly over the famed waiting room of Grand Central Terminal. Only a month before, the terminal had been declared a landmark by the city's Landmarks Preservation Commission (founded in 1965 to preserve buildings of historic or architectural significance). The British developer Morris Saady next leased the air rights over the terminal for fifty years at three million dollars per year. He hired the distinguished architect Marcel Breuer to build him a tower. Breuer proposed to float a fifty-five-story concrete slab over the station.[26] As Ada Louise Huxtable, *New York Times* architecture critic, pointed out, more than anything, the tower symbolized "the awesome value of New York air rights." Had it not been for the enormous value of the air, the tower project probably never would have come up. "That solid gold air is there to stay," Huxtable concluded, "and if its superheated values continue to rise as anticipated in the coming half century Manhattan could someday replace Fort Knox."[27]

Breuer himself would have rather demolished the terminal. But the landmarks commission prohibited that; nor did it favor his plan for cantilevering the tower over the building since it affected the exterior of the historic structure. So instead Breuer proposed a second tower that would have completely destroyed the terminal's exterior but saved the main concourse inside. "There has always been some question in the minds of informed people," said Breuer, "as to whether the exterior of Grand Central Terminal is worth preserving."[28] Again, the landmarks commission turned down the plan. "To protect a landmark," their report reads, "one does not tear it down. To perpetuate its architectural features, one does not strip them off."[29]

If only the railroad could have transferred its air rights somewhere else in the city, perhaps Grand Central would be spared the wrecking ball. Let the railroad realize the value of its air and maybe it would leave the terminal alone. Transferring air was nothing new in New York. The city had permitted the shifting of air rights from lot to lot to build higher towers at various times since the 1920s.[30] But starting in the 1960s, air rights were used to save the city's historic landmarks. Destruction was only one end to which the buying and selling of air might lead. Oddly enough, preservation was another. Because of changes in the zoning law, which we will address in a moment, the same air responsible for the destruction of the old buildings could instead be used to keep intact the city's architectural heritage. Maybe Marx was wrong. Maybe he had it backward when he said that things solid would melt into air. Maybe a way had been found for air to be used to give New Yorkers something solid to latch onto, a monumental remembrance of things past.

Using air rights transfers to preserve landmarks like Grand Central had its roots in a zoning law passed in 1961. New York needed a new zoning code at that time for one simple reason: Were building to take place in accordance with the 1916 resolution, the city would eventually have more than fifty million residents, not to mention a working population roughly the size of the entire United States today.[31] So to limit density, the law established floor area ratios (FARs) for all parts of the city. Consider this example. Suppose an area of the city was mapped with an FAR of eight. This meant that a builder with a zoning lot measuring ten thousand square feet could erect a structure containing no more than eighty thousand square feet of floor space on the site. To build twice as high, the builder could use only half the area of the lot.

Now nothing is more likely to cause apoplexy in a developer than a limit on building bulk. So to win support from the real estate community for the 1961 zoning resolution, concessions were made. Technically no area of the city was to have an FAR higher than fifteen; but by leaving room for a public plaza around the building, a 20 percent FAR bonus was added. Even more bulk could be squeezed onto the site by virtue of a second concession to development interests. The 1961 law liberalized the definition of the term "zoning lot." The term now included not just the building site but any other piece of land under identical ownership within the same city block. A lease of seventy-five years constituted "ownership" for zoning purposes. The rule allowed a developer to rent a vacant city parcel, thereby expanding the size of his zoning lot; this permitted the transfer of unused air rights over the empty land to the site of the new project.[32]

Grand Central Terminal's FAR was one and a half; the district's maximum FAR was eighteen, making for an enormous unused development potential. Were it not for the fact that Grand Central already occupied an entire zoning lot, the 1961 law might have helped the railroad with its unused air rights. Neither did a 1968 amendment to the zoning code aid the company, an unfortunate development since it was designed specifically to facilitate the transfer of air rights over landmarks. The new amendment expanded the definition of a contiguous parcel of land; now lots that were across the street from landmarks could qualify as designated receiving sites for unused air rights. Under the new amendment, transfers could also take place between lots owned separately so long as the shifted air rights did not exceed 20 percent of the bulk allowed on the site.[33] The idea behind the amendment was to help the financially strapped city preserve landmarks—to put an end to the fast-forward history of our demolition expert, Mr. Glick. Since the city could not afford to save anywhere near the number of landmarks worth saving by purchasing them, the zoning amendment let the owners of landmarks themselves do the preservation work. The amendment established transferable development rights (TDRs) in air which permitted landmark owners to sell the air and keep the historic building intact.[34] But again, the railroad could not reap any benefit from the zoning law change; all the newly defined "adjacent" lots were already fully developed.

Then in 1969, on precisely the day that the Penn Central company was readying to sue the city—for unconstitutionally taking its property in forbidding it to build its tower—the city planning commission proposed yet another amendment to the zoning code.[35] This one was tailor-made for the railroad. Again, the definition of an adjacent lot was broadened to include lots that were "across a street and opposite to another lot or lots which except for the intervention of streets or street intersections form a series extending to the lot occupied by the landmark building."[36] That was another way of simply saying that Grand Central's air rights could now take a cab uptown. The new amendment allowed the railroad to transfer its unused development rights five blocks north of the terminal to the Barclay Hotel on Lexington Avenue and Forty-eighth Street. Also, the 20 percent limit on the amount of air rights that could be transferred was rescinded. In effect, the new amendment amounted to an FAR windfall; it boosted the total FAR on the Barclay site to thirty-four and a half, just shy of *twice* the allowable maximum under the law.

But the railroad was still unhappy. In the time it took the planning commission to come up with a zoning code that fit its needs, the market for office space in New York had dampened considerably. "You don't make the market," developer Harry Helmsley said at the time. "The market makes you."[37] Penn Central chose to sue, not build. It launched a suit against the city alleging damages of eight million dollars a year until the tower over the terminal could be built.

It took almost a decade for the case to be settled. The railroad complained that the application of the landmarks law amounted to an unconstitutional taking of private property without just compensation. In the company's view, its property consisted of two parts: ground (the surface plus the underground terminal) and airspace. By dividing the property in such a way, the railroad was able to claim that it had been deprived the profitable use of its air rights, whatever value it still derived from the terminal itself. As events unfolded, the New York Supreme Court found for the company; the appellate court above, reversed; the state's highest court affirmed the reversal. On appeal to the U.S. Supreme Court, the decision against the railroad was reaffirmed in 1978. Justice William Brennan wrote the majority opinion. He held that the landmarks law did not amount to a taking. His reasoning was simple enough. Unlike the railroad, Brennan refused to divide the property into ground and airspace. His was a somewhat less modern concept of property than the railroad's (at least when it came to takings law). Call it premodern. " 'Taking' jurisprudence," he wrote, "does not divide a single parcel into discrete segments and attempt to determine whether rights in a particular segment have been entirely abrogated." It was the "parcel as a whole" that concerned him. Since the law forbidding the tower did not directly affect the company's ability to gainfully use the terminal, which it been doing for decades, no taking had occurred.[38]

Grand Central was saved. And yet the ruling did more than affirm the constitutionality of the landmarks law; it also established the value of transferable development rights in airspace. If Justice Brennan was not thinking entirely in three dimensions, there is no doubt that the decision sanctioned the exchange value of air rights. The city's TDR program for preserving landmarks—embodied in the amendments to the zoning law—was not yet perfect, the court opined. But *had* a taking occurred, the right to shift air rights to another parcel of land would have "undoubtedly mitigate[d] whatever financial burdens" the landmarks law imposed. If not quite *just* compensation for the taking of private property, TDRs were still compensation, said the court; ergo, TDRs in airspace were a valuable form of property.[39]

The preservation-minded hailed the decision as an important victory. "Today's ruling upholding the landmark law and preserving the integrity of Grand Central Station can truly be called a landmark decision," said New York's mayor, Ed Koch. There were others, of course, who were far less enthusiastic. Developer Melvyn Kaufman, whose family had been in the building business for six decades, said the decision would have important consequences for construction in the city. "It's not going to come cheap," he remarked. "There are no free lunches and the public will have to pay for it. Buildings that should be 30 stories tall will have to be 60."[40]

Meanwhile, as the Penn Central case worked its way through the courts, the zoning law was further amended. Until 1970, the law allowed the transfer of air rights only over privately owned landmarks. But what about publicly owned ones like the massive U.S. Custom House on lower Broadway, with its more than three quarters of a million square feet of unused airspace? A company wanted to demolish a fifteen-story building across Bowling Green and erect a fifty-story skyscraper in its place; but it did not have the necessary air rights to do so. The Custom House did. The planning commission helped by amending the zoning law to allow such a transfer, but the weak market in office space scuttled the deal. The Landmarks Preservation Commission favored the air rights amendment, although one commission member, Beverly Spatt, did speak out against it: "If we sell the air rights over the Custom House the first time, what will be next? The Public Library on 42d Street? And the museums?"[41]

As late as the early eighties, one could count the number of landmarks saved through air rights transfers on one hand.[42] There are too few fingers on the other hand to tally all the remaining air rights ventures that benefited solely private investors: Olympic Tower, Trump Tower, and the Tishman-Speyer building, just to name a few of the more notable ones.[43] What then should we conclude about the city's effort to use air rights to preserve the past? TDRs in airspace are a market solution to a market problem. They are premised on the idea that the exchange value of a landmark's air rights will be something that a nearby developer might want. If the real estate market is soft, as it often is, the value of the air diminishes, and so does the hope of saving the landmark.

Professor Lefebvre, whom we encountered earlier, has had something interesting to say about so-called solutions—like TDRs in airspace—to urban problems. Lefebvre, who, it may be relevant to point out, spent two years as a Paris cab driver, wrote as follows: "The supposed solutions of the planners . . . impose the constraints of exchangeability on everyday life, while presenting them as both natural (or normal) and technical requirements—and often also as moral necessities."[44] They are, in fact, none of the above. Solutions like TDRs to preserve landmarks are not simply neutral social practices; they are ideologies. While claiming to solve some problems, they force the ideology of exchange further into the marrow of daily existence.

To drive this point home, it is instructive to look at one air rights venture in more detail. The deal we are interested in involved the Racquet and Tennis Club, a Renaissance-style palazzo where the wealthy have gone to play squash and court tennis since 1918. The building is just up the block from Grand Central Terminal, at Park Avenue and Fifty-second Street. Built by McKim, Mead, and White, the five-story building did not achieve landmark status until after the events described below. But what happened at the

Racquet and Tennis Club has something to tell us about the relationship between air and preservation.

The story begins in 1969.[45] That is when the Fisher family—parvenus headed by Larry Fisher, who was once described as "a tough, audacious street fighter"—launched a new project. The Fisher Brothers have been in the building business since before the turn of the century. In 1974, five years and twenty-two million dollars later, Larry Fisher and family controlled a prime piece of Manhattan real estate in the middle of the block bounded by Park and Madison, between Fifty-second and Fifty-third. The site was perfect for an office tower. The Fishers needed two things from the Racquet and Tennis Club: air rights and its Park Avenue entrance, to give the new tower a fancy enough address to attract tenants. So in 1977 the Fisher Brothers offered the club a few hundred thousand dollars. The offer was rejected when Jonathan Morse, an architect, real estate developer, and club member, convinced the club's president that it was a lousy deal. Morse said he knew little about the matter but was quite frank in his opinion of the Fishers. "If Fisher Brothers was going to deal with the Racquet Club," he remarked, "then the Racquet Club was going to get screwed."

Unable to get the club to cooperate, the Fisher Brothers hatched a scheme to bring Park Avenue to them. They had their lawyer persuade the Manhattan borough president to change the address of their proposed building to "Park Avenue Plaza." The new address sounded fancy enough, even if it was not actually on Park Avenue. Now the Fishers no longer needed a right-of-way through the club. Nor did they need its air rights because of a special zoning bonus. Fisher Brothers had their architects design a huge, sixty-foot lobby for the building that would function as a public space. The lobby accomplished two things. It gave all the building's rental office space unobstructed views over the Racquet and Tennis Club. And, more important, it allowed the new tower an air rights bonus. The fact that the lobby would be open to the public qualified the building for an air rights increase equal to what the club had to offer. The Fisher Brothers would get their tower; the club would get nothing.

Unlike the Fishers, the Racquet and Tennis Club membership is old money—money that was not made by allowing people to take advantage of them. If the Fisher Brothers did not want their air, fine. They would use it themselves. Architects designed a hotel tower thirty-eight stories high to be cantilevered over the club. Throughout 1978, improvements were made to the design, including a plan by the architect Wally Rutes to increase the number of hotel rooms. (Rutes, according to Morse, had "a ton of concrete under his belt.") The hotel tower was supposed to save the building by helping the Racquet and Tennis Club to survive financially. But one solid reason for the hotel was to obstruct the Fisher Brothers—literally. If the hotel were built, the Fishers' tenants would gaze out their Park Avenue windows on a blank wall of concrete and steel.

In other words, the club was playing chicken, threatening to destroy itself in order to force the Fishers, now faced with an obstructed view, to buy its air rights. The club's scheme to shoehorn a huge tower over it was just like the plan to build a skyscraper over Grand Central. Some years back, when word of the Grand Central tower surfaced, the city's preservation commission suddenly became interested in making the building a landmark. And that was precisely what happened here. In the spring of 1978, the commission zeroed in on the Racquet and Tennis Club. Since it was very unlikely that the club's tower would be allowed once the building was designated a landmark, Morse and others tried to stall the preservation commission. As Morse put it, "It is not landmarking that makes it possible to preserve a building; it is the money that makes that building economically viable."

The club, of course, was bluffing all along. Yet so real, authentic, and absolutely viable was the club's plan for the hotel tower that even the savvy Fishers fell for the ruse. In August 1978, the Fisher Brothers capitulated. Convinced that the club might really build the hotel, the Fishers agreed to pay five million dollars for the air rights. One year earlier they had been willing to pay only three hundred thousand. The five million dollars, not landmarking, Morse pointed out, is what really saved the club.

What difference would it have made if the club had been declared a landmark? Probably none. In all likelihood, Park Avenue Plaza, as the Fishers' new tower was called, would have been built anyway (although the club no doubt would have received less money for the air rights). And if not Park Avenue Plaza, some other towering steel structure somewhere nearby would have gone up instead. Perhaps the New York skyline would look a little different today. But my question is this: How is it possible to talk about preserving anything in the superheated world of modern property values? What painfully few possibilities there are to save any building—landmark or not—when the sky is sliced up into three-dimensional pieces of property and regularly sold to generate greater profits. Keep in mind that the club was saved only when it threatened to destroy itself by putting a huge mass of steel overhead. That is an odd way to go about saving something. "In Manhattan's Culture of Congestion," writes Rem Koolhaas, "destruction is another word for preservation."[46] The reverse, we shall see shortly, is also true.

"SELL A COUNTRY!" exclaimed the Shawnee Indian chief Tecumseh in 1810. "Why not sell the air, the clouds

MORSE HOLDING PROPOSED HOTEL. RACQUET CLUB
AND PARK AVENUE PLAZA IN BACKGROUND

and the great sea, as well as the earth?"[47] Why not indeed. Tecumseh was far more prescient than he ever could have imagined.

The Shawnee chief died in 1813. But had he lived into the twentieth century, no doubt he never would have believed the air rights deal that resulted in the colossal Trump Tower, finished in 1983. One can just picture the amazement on Tecumseh's face as he stared up at the sleek, sixty-eight-story glass ziggurat. Beneath the glass—with its twenty-eight sides—are ninety thousand tons of reinforced concrete, one of the tallest such concrete structures on the face of the earth. The words "Trump Tower" in bronze letters two feet high are emblazoned over the Fifth Avenue entrance. Inside is a huge atrium with a waterfall and public garden encased in more than two hundred tons of imported Italian marble; plenty of the world's most expensive retail stores selling everything from designer baby shoes to gold watches; thirteen floors of office space; and over two hundred fifty condominiums. When it opened a decade ago, a one-bedroom condo sold for half a million dollars. On the elevator going up we explain to the chief that Tiffany, in the building next door, sold its air rights totaling five million dollars to Donald Trump, who parlayed them into this sawtoothed colossus.

If Trump Tower were a person, its diagnosis would be narcissistic personality disorder. It stands as a symbol of the American Dream come true. You can shop at the best stores the world has to offer; live, if you can afford it, in one of the tallest residential towers offering stunning views of the city; rub elbows with the stars, including Johnny Carson, Steven Spielberg, and Paul Anka, not to mention Donald Trump himself, who lives—where else?—in the penthouse, replete with an eighty-foot living room. "In America," Mayor Koch said at the tower's topping-off party, "if you have your own dollars you're allowed to build what you want."[48] That was a stunning statement coming from the city's highest official; but who had time to bother with zoning laws or other nonsense? Let the party begin. Trump had built his monument.

Trump Tower is more than just a towering symbol of twentieth-century materialism; it also symbolizes air's transformation into a commodity. For Donald Trump, bigger is always better. And that was precisely the logic that informed this project from the very start. "Size," as he put it some years later, "was a top priority."[49] Trump began in 1979 by buying the Bonwit Teller Building on Fifth Avenue and Fifty-sixth Street, a stately Art Deco structure made of limestone. Then he negotiated an agreement with Equitable Life, which owned the land underneath the site. But the key to the tower project was the Tiffany air rights. Using just the Bonwit site alone, Trump's architect, Der Scutt, estimated that a building with a maximum FAR of eight and a half could be built.[50] That translated into twenty stories with roughly two hundred thousand square feet of space. However, purchasing the air rights over the Tiffany building boosted the possible floor space by 50 percent. By the time he was through—buying air rights, assembling land, and, by his own admission, twisting the arm of the city planning commission into allowing him a bigger building—Trump had extracted a maximum FAR of twenty-one from the site.[51] It amounted to enough floor space to give him the sixty-eight-story tower he was after.

According to Trump, when he sat down with Walter Hoving of Tiffany to negotiate the air rights, he told him, "I'm offering you five million dollars . . . to let me preserve Tiffany. In return you're selling me something—air rights—that you'd never use anyway."[52] It was hard to quarrel with that logic. And Tiffany is still there on Fifth Avenue, to this very day, as proof of Trump's sincerity. The Bonwit Teller Building is gone, of course. If you call that preservation-minded, then consider Trump's treatment of the two bas-relief sculptures on the face of the old Bonwit building. Trump first promised them to the Metropolitan Museum of Art. But when he realized that properly removing the pieces would cost him half a million dollars, he had them jack-hammered. Thus, in the words of Robert Miller, owner of an art gallery across the street from Bonwit, "Trump destroyed the past to put his belligerent mark on the future."[53]

Trump Tower may not be a typical New York City air rights deal, but we can learn from it nonetheless. From Trump's perspective, he was carrying out his duty as a modern-day developer, treating airspace as an instrumentality to build bigger and to realize greater profits. But the commodification of airspace also needs to be seen in historical perspective. Since the seventeenth century, Americans have been slowly transforming the earth—land, trees, water, fish, livestock, grain, and so on— into a set of commodities. The commodity we now call airspace is of a piece with this particular way of conversing with the planet. It is a mistake to think that it was inevitable—"a matter of time"—before airspace too would fall victim to capitalist property. Things did not have to turn out this way; Grand Central's air rights did not have to be leased; the zoning law did not have to permit air rights transfers; Trump Tower did not have to be built to such a height. Of course, that is all the world that could have been but is not. In the real world of twentieth-century New York, airspace has been pulverized; space has been brought, in the words of the geographer David Harvey, "under the single measuring rod of money value."[54] Nothing was more critical to the commodification of airspace than the rise of three-dimensional property. It was the language of property that made it possible to own and hence to exchange airspace freely. The symbolic technology of three-dimensional property—with its deterritorialized vision of real estate, its zoning boxes, and floor area ratios—allowed developers and lawyers to invest airspace with value, to conquer, own, and trade it.

And trade it they did. The Trump project marked the beginning of another New York building boom. Between 1979 and 1987, when the stock market crashed, developers redesigned Manhattan. Fifty-nine new office buildings alone went up, containing over thirty-eight million square feet of space, the equivalent of twenty-seven more Empire State Buildings. "In the last five years," reported the *New York Times* in 1986, Manhattan's developers "have moved so much air around, stacked it so high in such slender columns and then built within it that they have redrawn the skyline."[55]

One of the more grandiose air rights ventures from this period is the CitySpire tower. The tower was the work of Bruce Eichner, developer and Harvard Business School graduate. Back in 1983, Eichner visited a dilapidated garage on West Fifty-sixth Street. On that site, he dreamed himself a tower thirty-four stories tall. Then he took a stroll around the block. What he found was the dilapidated City Center Theater. Once before, the city had sold air rights over one of its buildings. So Eichner negotiated a deal with the city to contribute six million dollars, half to the opera and half to the ballet. Culture in the city profited, and so, of course, did Eichner. The deal gave him enough air rights to build an additional twenty-six stories. By agreeing to contribute another five and a half million dollars to help renovate the theater itself (the zoning law allowed such a bonus), Eichner gained twelve more stories. When he was through he had built the city's highest residential building (one story higher than Trump Tower). "The land has expandable possibilities," Eichner remarked. "But you have to figure out creative ways to see value."[56]

The eighties, that decade of unbridled capitalist optimism and entrepreneurial ambition, saw developers prowling all over the city in search of potential cash-register towers.[57] The city's churches, which tended to be built just a few stories high, came under particular scrutiny. In 1982, Rev. Evert Olson of the Church of Sweden sold the air rights over his four-story church on Forty-eighth Street for nearly a million dollars. "We hardly believed it," Christine Olson, the pastor's wife remarked. "In Sweden they just shook their heads and said it must be a miracle. Such things don't happen there."[58] But in New York, the miracle of turning air into cash occurred with some regularity.

Probably the most controversial air rights venture ever involved Park Avenue's famed St. Bartholomew's Church. Early in the eighties, the developer Howard Ronson revealed a plan to demolish the community house attached to the church and build a tower fifty-nine stories tall to cantilever over the church's beautiful Byzantine dome. The financially strapped church claimed it needed to sell the air rights for the tower to preserve itself. St. Bartholomew's Church had already been declared a landmark, so it needed permission from the city to build a tower that might affect its exterior. Had the possible receiving sites in the neighborhood not already been fully developed, St. Bart's might have been able to transfer its unused air rights elsewhere. Its leaders said the church had no choice but to let the tower be built. "The Christian church must be free to carry out the commands laid upon us by Jesus Christ," said Paul

Moore, Jr., bishop of New York. "St. Bartholomew's seeks to carry out its ministry under those commands and cannot do so unless a secure new source of revenue can be found." Put simply: God Almighty demanded the tower. The plan raised a tidal wave of opposition from architecture critics, lawyers, planners, and churchgoers themselves. One theologically minded observer put it this way: "We know that heaven is not literally up. But modern man still considers that his prayers fly up. The idea that they would do so through desks, chairs, wastebaskets and ashtrays would be something of an anticlimax."[59]

The landmarks commission turned down the tower plan. A second tower designed to forty-seven stories—described by one opponent as "monstrous, needle-esque"—was also rejected. Rebuffed twice, the church took its case all the way to the U.S. Supreme Court. In 1991, the court stayed the wrecking ball by refusing to hear the case. "We're disappointed, of course," explained senior warden Fletcher Hodges III. "Our next step will be looking into long-term fund-raising programs."[60]

The threat of a tower over St. Bart's stands as a negative symbol of where the freedom to buy and sell three-dimensional property might take us. What the church sought in its tower scheme was something that most property owners want at one time or another: the freedom to do as they pleased with what was theirs. Yet as Lefebvre once observed, private property involves privation.[61] In this case, the church was seeking to deprive itself, its members, the world, of the past to realize a new future of towering steel and glass. There may be something to recommend such a future. Certainly the developer himself would benefit; the church too would gain financially. Perhaps some of that newfound wealth extracted from the sky's frontier might even dribble down to the poor and homeless found crawling up Park Avenue. But before we build any more such capitalist cathedrals, we should stop and rethink our priorities.

Airspace is unique in that it presents few problems compared to owning, say, underground water or land along a river. Airspace is an abstraction. And abstractions, because they are human artifacts, tend to be easier to own since, unlike land or water, we humans invented them. All that needed to happen was for the law of property to define airspace as a thing that was real enough to be owned. It is a tribute to the colonizing impulse at the heart of property law that it has been able to encroach on the space above the earth. Of course, the urban consequences of modern three-dimensional real estate might be something to question: the increasing density in the fashionable midtown area, the wind, the noise, the loss of sunlight. But consequences of a different sort are what concern us now. A world where virtually everything—airspace included—is transformed into property and exchanged is, to be sure, a very creative world. It is also an impoverished, even dangerous world as well, full of lots of fast-moving history. Recall that to preserve itself, the church was saying, it needed to destroy its architectural past. All it had come to mean to its parishioners and others—passersby wandering up Park Avenue, whoever—would come crashing down so the church could be saved. Saved? One wonders about the sanity of a culture in which the goal of preservation is reached only through destruction.

Paper Moon:
A Conclusion

There is real estate and unreal estate.
—DON DELILLO (1987)

Robert Heinlein always did have quite an imagination. In his 1950 science fiction classic, *The Man Who Sold the Moon*, Heinlein introduces us to that tireless lunarphile cum entrepreneur, D. D. Harriman. For Harriman, who is inclined toward the grandiose, building a spaceship and sending it to the moon is just the beginning. What he is really after is nothing short of "the greatest real estate venture since the Pope carved up the New World." "I want to sell land on the Moon," says Harriman. "I'll sell the whole Moon, if I can—surface rights, mineral rights, anything."[1]

Step one for Harriman and his space age business partner, George Strong, is to figure out exactly who owns the earth's only satellite. "If basic law says that a man owns the wedge of sky above his farm out to infinity," Harriman asks Strong, "*who owns the Moon?*" According to Harriman's calculations, the moon swings over a belt of land twenty-nine degrees north and south of the equator. "If one man owned all that belt of Earth—it's roughly the tropical zone—then he'd own the Moon, too, wouldn't he?" But Strong is dubious; owning the moon is like trying to own "a migrating goose," he says. Harriman:

And nobody has title to a migrating bird. I get your point—but the Moon *always* stays over that one belt. If you move a boulder in your garden, do you lose title to it? Is it still real estate? Do the title laws still stand? This is like that group of real estate cases involving wandering islands in the Mississippi, George— the land moved as the river cut new channels, *but somebody always owned it*. In this case I plan to see to it that we are the "somebody."[2]

As the saying goes, truth is stranger than fiction. In 1955, Robert Coles, president of the Interplanetary Development Corporation, offered investors quitclaim deeds to one-acre plots of prime bottomland. Location: Copernicus Crater, northeast quadrant, the moon. Mary Pierce, for one, admitted being rather shocked by the whole idea. She was the Glen Cove city clerk when Coles walked into her Long Island office and filed papers incorporating his new company. In those papers Coles swore that since no one had ever claimed the moon, he was doing so for real estate purposes. A mere dollar entitled buyers to an acre of land, mineral rights, and "the right to fish, dredge and clam in, upon and under the Sea of Nectar."[3]

This was not the first time that the Coles family had ventured into real estate. Back in the seventeenth century, Mr. Coles's ancestors stepped ashore on Long Island, headed straight into the wilderness, and made history by becoming the first settlers of Glen Cove. So Coles was no stranger to uncharted terrain. The consummate Renaissance man— astronomer, historian, naturalist, author, educator—Coles briefly attended Columbia University, served as chairman of the Hayden Planetarium, and even had his own radio show. Now the host of radio's "This Wonderful World" was selling property that was literally out of this world. What was the Hayden's response to their former chairman's scheme? "Mr. Coles is no longer associated with the Planetarium."[4]

To be fair, Coles was only offering to sell the side of the moon that faced the earth. "We wouldn't sell land we'd never seen," he said.[5] And sell he did to, among others, Howard Brandy of New York City, who sent for five acres so long as the land would allow him to park his "Ford Thunderbird on an even surface." Sarah Morton of St. Louis took the moon rush more seriously: "It will really make me enjoy our lovely moon 10 times more if I know I own two acres up there," she remarked.[6] At one point there were more than four thousand such investors in Coles's scheme.

Oddly enough, Coles was not alone in the lunar realty business. Also involved in selling property on the moon was Harry Hall, an insurance agent from Miami Beach. Founder of the Lunar Fantasy Corporation, Hall claimed title to the entire moon, not just the side facing the earth. "If he gets there first and stakes out lots, okay," responded Coles. "But if we get there first we're going to substantiate our claim."[7]

A few years before Coles's moon offering, a New York lawyer named Oscar Schachter in an article entitled "Who Owns the Universe?" wrote as follows: "We have all heard about attempts to sell real estate on the moon and have laughed at the poor suckers who bit . . . but now that scientists have shown that man can conquer space and that new worlds lie within his reach, the question of 'owning' the moon and the planets no longer seems to be such a joke."[8] Was Coles kidding or not? For his part, Coles was clear

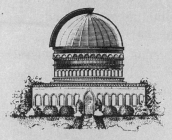

INTERPLANETARY
DEVELOPMENT
CORPORATION

A Profit Corporation
Dedicated to

EXPLORATION OF PLANETS
PUBLIC EDUCATION
DEVELOPMENT OF SATELLITES

AND SIMILAR ACTIVITIES

ALSO ROCKETS

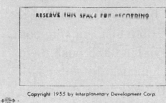

RESERVE THIS SPACE FOR RECORDING

Copyright 1955 by Interplanetary Development Corp.

Title No. B 05510

General Quitclaim
DEED
to
ONE ACRE
OF LAND
on the
MOON
(NORTHEAST QUADRANT)

**INTERPLANETARY
DEVELOPMENT
CORPORATION**

LUNAR LUNACY

about his intentions: "We are not trying to put anything over on anybody. Anybody who's half-intelligent who reads the deed will realize it's a joke."[9] But the state attorney general's office was not so sure. Assistant Attorney General Leonard E. Russack told a reporter, "I really can't judge this situation . . . but from what you tell me it sounds very grotesque, indeed. You may rest assured that I am going to look into it."[10] According to one report, 90 percent of the letters sent to Coles indicated that buyers realized he was jesting. Of course, such a joke was only funny to a culture willing to go to almost any length to own land. An acre in Copernicus Crater, wrote Ken Wagner in the *American Mercury*, was "the perfect gift for people who 'have everything.'"[11] It was also the perfect scheme for a culture that, given the opportunity, wanted to own everything.

Mr. Coles, it is worth noting, was said to be a great admirer of none other than Mark Twain.[12] Indeed, Coles's joke on the American public is much like the one Twain describes involving Buncombe, the gullible U.S. attorney, who took the "judge" seriously in the farcical Slide Mountain case. Both of these jokes work because they are caricatures of the real world of property. Both take our common cultural understandings of property in land and push them to their logical, but absurd, conclusion. And in both cases there are some people who fall for the gag, who do not get the joke. In the domain of real property there is always the risk of being had.

But notice how much further Coles must go to make us laugh. The two stories are amusing because they verge on being plausible. Only in the time between Twain and Coles, the boundary of plausibility has shifted outward—some two hundred thousand miles from the earth. What it is plausible to own has grown so much over the course of the twentieth century that Coles has to go awfully far for the joke to be effective.

Nineteen fifty-seven. Just two years later and no one was laughing. In the wake of the Russians' successful *Sputnik* launch, who owned the moon became a far more serious question. The moon was the ultimate Loose-Fish—as Herman Melville might have said—just waiting to be caught. Let the Soviets establish first possession of the satellite, reasoned some Americans, and they could claim ownership over it.[13] Andrew G. Haley, space law expert and president of the International Astronautical Federation, put it simply: "If the Russians get to the moon first, they can claim it. If we get there first, we can. This is my opinion."[14]

The Russians got there first. They sent up an eight-hundred-pound metal sphere and thirty-five hours later on September 14, 1959, it came crashing down on the moon. It was the first object ever sent from one celestial body to another, and it was a far-reaching achievement. (Reacting to the moon shot, rainmaker Wallace Howell said, "It's as if they had hit the Washington Monument without touching a single Government office building.")[15] But the Soviets did not just send a rocket to the moon. They sent a rocket bearing pennants inscribed with the Soviet coat of arms, the notorious hammer and sickle. That could mean only one thing to American observers: the Soviets were trying to lay claim to the earth's only satellite.

Even before the space rocket landed, the specter of a red moon was raised. One newspaper story began, "If the Soviet Union has landed its flag on the moon, does that give Moscow prime claim to authority over the lunar sphere?" Sen. Mike Mansfield thought that "technically" it would, but since "nobody is accompanying the flag," any territorial claim would be open to question.[16] The day the rocket actually did hit the moon, the United States announced that it rejected any legal claim based on the planting of Soviet flags. And so, for his part, did Robert Coles. "A rocket can't do anything about the real estate up there," he remarked, "and until they put a man up there to stake out claims, our holdings are still good."[17] In fact, the Soviet leadership denied any such claim to possession resulting from the rocket hit.[18]

Meanwhile, U.S. Rep. Victor Anfuso of Brooklyn, at the time on a mission to Moscow to promote the peaceful use of outer space, commented, "If we were the first to land on the moon . . . we would hoist not our banner and claim it for ourselves, but claim it for all the world as a new achievement of Earthmen."[19] Ten years later when the United States did land on the moon, Neil Armstrong claimed it for the world; then he planted an American flag to prove it.[20] By then, however, the United States had signed an international accord that prevented any nation from claiming sovereignty over the satellite. So selling real estate there was out of the question. But that did not stop the *National Review* from writing, in all seriousness, as follows: "A successful moon landing this month will open a whole new field of law, as the question must be answered, under emerging interplanetary real estate law, who 'owns' the moon?"[21] Is there nothing that stands outside the realm of real property? If lunar realty can be entertained as serious or even half-serious, what better evidence is there of property's transcendental status, an institution so all-encompassing, limitless, and absolute that nothing exists beyond its grasp, not even the moon. In modern America, possession seems to know few limits.[22]

In the time between Twain and this lunacy, the idea of property evolved toward an ever-greater level of abstraction.

It did so, as mentioned earlier, partly to encompass the new forms of wealth created by corporate capitalism. Property, which was once considered simply a thing, evolved to take into account stocks, bonds, trademarks, and business goodwill. It was a claim on the market value of something that defined one's property interest in it. "Property," wrote Justice Noah H. Swayne in the famous *Slaughterhouse Cases* of 1873, "is everything which has exchangeable value."[23] So as the twentieth century progressed and additional sources of value—newly created land, underground water, air—were uncovered through technological change, property law evolved to help bring these new resources into the world of market relations. The concept of property became more abstract, and it became so in order to reduce the earth, in all its complexity, into a set of ownable things. Put simply, property law evolved in a way that helped turn more and more of the planet into less and less, benefiting fewer and fewer.

But it may be wrong to say that property law *evolved*. It was not evolution so much as *involution* that was happening. In 1936, the American anthropologist Alexander Goldenweiser proposed the latter concept. By involution he meant to describe what happened when a cultural form (art, ritual, and music were his examples) developed in such a way that it became increasingly complex, yet at the same time rigid, monotonous, and unable to change in any fundamental sense. Here, for example, is what Goldenweiser had to say about Maori art.

[It is] distinguished by its complexity, elaborateness, and the extent to which the entire decorated object is pervaded by the decoration. On analysis the unit elements of the design are found to be few in number; in some instances, in fact, the complex design is brought about through a multiplicity of spatial arrangements of one and the same unit. What we have here is a pattern plus continued development. . . . The inevitable result is progressive complication, variety within uniformity, virtuosity within monotony. This is *involution*.[24]

It was mainly "primitive" cultures that Goldenweiser had in mind when he spoke of involution, not his own twentieth-century America. But the concept works nicely there as well to describe what has happened to property law. Like Maori art, property too is a cultural form. It rests, as we have seen, on the ideas of ownership and possession, very old ideas, but ones that have grown all the more tenacious in our own century as they have been pressed hard to colonize the planet's more distant reaches. In the process, the law of property has grown all the more technically complicated and ornate. More than three thousand amendments were made to New York City's original zoning ordinance by the time it was replaced by a new law in 1961.[25] So much has been written about water law that the entry for the topic in one legal encyclopedia stretches to over one thousand pages; the index alone is almost one hundred pages long.[26] Property law is a vast exercise in what Goldenweiser called "technical hairsplitting." It is a virtuoso performance but also in many ways a rigid and dreary one that does not benefit everyone equally and, further, that may well hamper our future ability to adapt to changing environmental conditions.

And yet for all its technical complexity and inflexibility, for all its faults, it is still true that the law of property is one of the most important conversations we Americans have with the natural world. Property is one of the most powerful cultural forms for shaping our sense of place. It remains the privileged language for gaining control of nature, so privileged, in fact, that for many—developers, realtors, suburbanites—it is virtually the only way they know of relating to the environment. There is, of course, little question that in the majority of cases the law of property works quite well to help control and own the natural world. That alone explains its continued popularity. Still, it tends to break down at the margins when it tries to own every square inch of earth, every last drop of water. "It has been said that no definition of a natural watercourse can be given that will apply to all cases," writes our legal encyclopedia.[27] And what we cannot define, we cannot own—at least not as fully as we might like. But that has never stopped anyone from trying. Discover a new land, new resources with economic potential, and it is property law that we turn to to hold fast to that discovery.[28]

If there was one idea shared by all the participants in our stories—white speculators and Indians struggling to own land on the Great Plains through to New York developers turning a profit on air rights—it is that nature and the earth more generally should, must, be subject to ownership. Certainly there was disagreement over *who* ought to profit from the earth. But on one point, all would most likely nod their heads in approval: Everything must have an owner. That is a collective dream that, for all the problems and contradictions it raises, we keep trying to realize.

Even Henry David Thoreau, nature lover though he was, could not help dreaming about owning a slice of the earth he loved so much. Many times he imagined what it would be like to own land near his home at Walden Pond. He wandered the neighborhood, weighed the possibilities of each parcel, pictured in his mind what it would be like to live in one spot or another, to build a house, improve the land.

Then he ventured on before his fingers got "burned by actual possession." As he wrote, "Man is rich in proportion to the number of things which he can afford to let alone."[29] By Thoreau's standards, the modern American landscape is a very poor one indeed.

NOTES

Notes

DMR *Des Moines Register*

FCN *Fulton County News* (McConnellsburg, Pa.)

FD *Fulton Democrat* (McConnellsburg, Pa.)

NYT *New York Times*

SCJ *Sioux City Journal*

FAST FISH IN AMERICA: AN INTRODUCTION

1. Quoted material is from Mark Twain (Samuel L. Clemens), *Roughing It* (Hartford, Conn.: American Publishing Co., 1872), 245–246.

2. Marc Reisner, *Cadillac Desert: The American West and Its Disappearing Water* (1986; reprint, New York: Penguin Books, 1987), 506–510.

3. *Pierson* v. *Post*, 3 Cai. R. 175, 178 (N.Y. Sup. Ct. 1805). For a very brief history of the case, see James Truslow Adams, *Memorials of Old Bridgehampton* (1916; reprint, Port Washington, N.Y.: Ira J. Friedman, 1962), 66.

4. Carol M. Rose, "Possession as the Origin of Property," *University of Chicago Law Review* 52 (1985): 81. For more on possession, see Richard A. Epstein, "Possession as the Root of Title," *Georgia Law Review* 13 (1979): 1221–1243, and "Past and Future: The Temporal Dimension in the Law of Property," *Washington University Law Quarterly* 64 (1986): 667–722.

5. "Hard" here refers to hardship. In other words, if you make a fuss about individual hardship in a hard case, you are apt to make bad law in other cases where no such hardship exists. However, these days the phrase "hard case" is often used to mean tricky case and the saying is sometimes construed to mean that such tricky cases make bad law as well.

6. I refer here to the work of the anthropologist Roy Rappaport, who is not discussing the single-minded pursuit of property but rather the way that a large industrial firm might single-mindedly pursue its own interests through the government at the expense of the larger ecosystem. He gives as an example of this latter process the famous remark that the former president of General Motors, Charles Wilson, made when he was secretary of defense: "What is good for General Motors is good for America." "I would suggest," writes Rappaport, "that no matter how benign the purposes of General Motors may be, what is good for General Motors, or any such firm, cannot in the long run be good for America because for America to commit herself to what is good for General Motors is for America to sacrifice evolutionary flexibility, that is to say ability to adapt to circumstances continuously changing in ways that cannot be foreseen." See Roy A. Rappaport, "Nature, Culture, and Ecological Anthropol-

ogy," in *Man, Culture, and Society*, ed. Harry L. Shapiro, rev. ed. (London: Oxford Univ. Press, 1971), 263.

On the ecological impact of different forms of property ownership, Donald Worster notes the results of a 1936 Forest Service study of the western range. According to Worster, the worst ecological devastation took place on lands that were in the public domain. However, he also notes that it is surprising to learn that those rangelands owned by private landowners were in terrible ecological condition as well. Ownership of land in fee simple, in other words, seemed to offer landowners little incentive to use it in an ecologically sustainable fashion and indeed seemed to encourage precisely the opposite behavior: the short-term maximization of profits at the expense of ecology. See Donald Worster, "Cowboy Ecology," in *Under Western Skies: Nature and History in the American West* (New York: Oxford Univ. Press, 1992), 48.

7. Nor, of course, is this what most law professors mean when they talk about the term. Property law, one well-regarded casebook explains, "is concerned with relations among persons with respect to things." Charles M. Haar and Lance Liebman, *Property and Law* (Boston: Little, Brown and Co., 1977), 1.

8. C. B. Macpherson, ed., *Property: Mainstream and Critical Positions* (Toronto: Univ. of Toronto Press, 1978), 7. Also see Macpherson, "Capitalism and the Changing Concept of Property," in *Feudalism, Capitalism and Beyond*, ed. Eugene Kamenka and R. S. Neale (New York: St. Martin's Press, 1975), 104–124.

9. A. W. B. Simpson, *A History of the Land Law*, 2d ed. (Oxford: Clarendon Press, 1986), 88, 104. Although Simpson does not talk specifically about the meaning of the word *property*, he does note a tendency on the part of "medieval man" to treat "rights as *things*," in opposition to Macpherson's thoughts.

10. Macpherson, *Property*, 8.

11. John R. Stilgoe, "Jack o'lanterns to Surveyors: The Secularization of Landscape Boundaries," *Environmental Review* 1 (1976): 21.

12. See Simpson, *Land Law*, 85, where he notes that sometime near the end of the thirteenth century lawyers were "using the word 'estate' to describe the quantum of interest which a tenant has in his land."

13. J. A. Simpson and E. S. C. Weiner, comps., *The Oxford English Dictionary*, 2d ed. (Oxford: Clarendon Press, 1989), 5:407–408, 12:639–640. Although it is not until the eighteenth century that the word *property* meant a parcel of land, the dictionary does note evidence suggesting that the word signified a thing or possession as early as the fourteenth century.

14. E. P. Thompson, *Whigs and Hunters: The Origin of the Black Act* (New York: Pantheon, 1975), 207. However, Thompson seems to have underestimated the range of forces that inspired the Black Act. See, e.g., John Broad, "Whigs and Deer-Stealers in Other Guises: A Return to the Origins of the Black Act," *Past and Present* 119 (1988): 56–72.

15. William Blackstone, *Commentaries on the Laws of England*, 1st ed. (1765–1769; reprint, Chicago: Univ. of Chicago Press, 1979), 2:2.

16. Karl Marx, *Capital* (1867; reprint, New York: International Publishers, 1967), 1:72.

17. Hildegard Binder Johnson, *Order Upon the Land: The U.S. Rectangular Land Survey and the Upper Mississippi Country* (New York: Oxford Univ. Press, 1976), 40–42. The logic of the grid system rests on simple arithmetic. Each box measures six by six miles and is itself divided into thirty-six smaller boxes, one mile square. The grid's enormous power over nature becomes clear if we compare it to another somewhat less effective way of bounding the land. In much of the eastern part of the United States, from Maine south to Georgia, property boundaries were drawn according to the metes and bounds approach. This involved establishing a beginning point and then using directions and measurements to encompass a plot of land (commencing at some location, then north two hundred feet, and so on). It was critical, of course, to make sure that one began the description at some permanent location. But standards vary. "Commencing at a point on the River Road near the big hemlock tree where Philo Bates killed the bear," reads one land description from Maine. Another reads, "Commencing at the point where I, Joshua Colby, Justice of the Peace, stood at 3:30 p.m., April 17, 1830." (Quoted in R. P. Boyd and David L. Uelmen, "Re-Surveys and Metes and Bounds Descriptions," *Wisconsin Law Review* 1953 [1953]: 659.) Most of the time, the metes and bounds approach works well enough to establish one's claim to land. But there is no comparing it to the precision of the rectangular survey with its neatly numbered boxes. Thus was the land carved up over the course of the nineteenth century into numbered sections, townships, and ranges—divided, conquered, and sold to settlers as they pushed their way west.

18. Eric Foner, *Tom Paine and Revolutionary America* (New York: Oxford Univ. Press, 1976), 249.

19. William B. Scott, *In Pursuit of Happiness: American Conceptions of Property from the Seventeenth to the Twentieth Century* (Bloomington: Indiana Univ. Press, 1977), 58.

20. Quoted in Johnson, *Order Upon the Land*, 158. For an excellent discussion of how private property transformed the landscape of colonial America, see William Cronon, *Changes in the Land: Indians, Colonists, and the Ecology of New England* (New York: Hill and Wang, 1983), 54–81.

21. Thomas C. Grey, "The Disintegration of Property," in *NOMOS XXII: Property*, ed. J. Roland Pennock and John W. Chapman (New York: New York Univ. Press, 1980), 70; Kenneth J. Vandevelde, "The New Property of the Nineteenth Century: The Development of the Modern Concept of Property," *Buffalo Law Review* 29 (1980): 325–367.

22. See Charles A. Reich, "The New Property," *Yale Law Journal* 73 (1964): 733–787.

23. The use of the stick metaphor is suggestive in light of the very old custom of livery of seisin. This common law ceremony was performed when land was transferred and involved the grantor picking up a twig or clod of earth and delivering it to the grantee, the act signifying the delivery of possession to the new owner. Blackstone, *Commentaries*, 2:314.

24. Quoted in Morton J. Horwitz, *The Transformation of American Law, 1870–1960: The Crisis of Legal Orthodoxy* (New York: Oxford Univ. Press, 1992), 156. Also see the excellent discussion of the change to a more modern concept of property, 145–167.

25. See, e.g., Grey, "The Disintegration of Property," 69–85. Also see Bruce A. Ackerman, *Private Property and the Constitution* (New Haven: Yale Univ. Press, 1977), which explores in detail the incoherence of current thought on the compensation clause of the Constitution.

26. Here I am elaborating on the example offered in Grey, "The Disintegration of Property," 70–71.

27. Clifford Geertz, *Local Knowledge: Further Essays in Interpretive Anthropology* (New York: Basic Books, 1983), 173.

28. Evidence of the almost transcendental power of real estate can be found in the area of law known as conflict of laws. Put simply, these technical rules determine which body of law (say, as between two neighboring states) ought to be applied in a legal dispute. The twentieth century has seen the dissolution of stable rules for ad hoc analysis in virtually every area of law (torts, contracts) *but real property*, where the stability and the "thingness" of land has preserved the older system. Thus the law of situs of land—which holds that the applicable law governing descent or transfer is that of the state where the property is located—has remained remarkably unchanged to this day. See Russell J. Weintraub, *Commentary on the Conflict of Laws*, 3d ed. (Mineola, N.Y.: Foundation Press, 1986), 412–415; Eugene F. Scoles and Peter Hay, *Conflict of Laws*, 2d ed. (St. Paul: West Publishing, 1992), 743–745; and Herbert F. Goodrich, "Two States and Real Estate," *University of Pennsylvania Law Review* 89 (1941): 417–419.

29. Herman Melville, *Moby-Dick or the Whale*, ed. Willard Thorp (1851; reprint, New York: Oxford Univ. Press, 1947), 373–374.

1. BLACKBIRD'S GHOST:
REAL ESTATE AND OTHER FANTASIES

1. *Original Journals of the Lewis and Clark Expedition, 1804–1806*, ed. Reuben Gold Thwaites (New York: Dodd, Mead and Co., 1904–1905), 6:88.

Notes

2. The Omaha along with other tribes signed a treaty in 1836 which conveyed land east of the Missouri River.

3. G. Hubert Smith, *Omaha Indians: Ethnohistorical Report on the Omaha People* (New York: Garland, 1974), 80–81, 87–88, 93, 101–114.

4. Ibid., 93–95, 100, 120–123.

5. Treaty with the Omahas, Mar. 16, 1854, 10 Stat. 1043.

6. The act also gave single people over eighteen as well as orphans eighty acres. Those under eighteen were given forty. The act served as a model for the famous Dawes Severalty Act of 1887.

7. Quoted in Nancy Oestreich Lurie, "The Lady from Boston and the Omaha Indians," *American West* 3 (1966): 32, 33.

8. Alice C. Fletcher, "Lands in Severalty to Indians; Illustrated by Experiences with the Omaha Tribe," *Proceedings of the American Association for the Advancement of Science* 33 (1884): 657, 659–660.

9. Margaret Mead, *The Changing Culture of an Indian Tribe* (New York: Columbia Univ. Press, 1932), 55.

10. Lurie, "Lady from Boston," 82.

11. George Fitch, "The Missouri River: Its Habits and Eccentricities Described by a Personal Friend," *American Magazine* 63 (1907): 639.

12. Quoted in Marc Reisner, *Cadillac Desert: The American West and Its Disappearing Water* (1986; reprint, New York: Penguin Books, 1987), 191.

13. Michael L. Lawson, *Dammed Indians: The Pick-Sloan Plan and the Missouri River Sioux, 1944–1980* (Norman: Univ. of Oklahoma Press, 1982), 27.

14. "'Operation Bootstrap' at Macy," *SCJ*, May 17, 1970.

15. "Indians Occupy Land Near Onawa," *SCJ*, Apr. 6, 1973.

16. Quoted in "Claim to Accretion Land up for Study," *SCJ*, Sept. 4, 1967.

17. "Indians Again Occupy Farmland Near Onawa," *SCJ*, Apr. 5, 1975.

18. Quoted in "Iowa and Indian Tribe Fighting Bitter Land Dispute," *NYT*, Feb. 18, 1979.

19. Affidavit of Otis Peterson, Sept. 24, 1975, no. 40, p. 2, CP1.

20. Quoted in William Cronon, *Changes in the Land: Indians, Colonists, and the Ecology of New England* (New York: Hill and Wang, 1983), 56–57.

21. "He Faces Land Loss," *SCJ*, Apr. 30, 1978.

22. Quoted in "Judge Rules Against Indians in Bid for Iowa Land on Missouri River," *DMR*, May 5, 1977.

23. Quoted in "Tribe's Battle for Blackbird Bend Not Over," *DMR*, June 4, 1987.

24. Quoted in "The Tragedy of Blackbird Bend," *DMR*, Jan. 21, 1979.

25. Both quotations are from "The Tragedy of Blackbird Bend," *DMR*, Jan. 21, 1979.

26. It was Alice Fletcher who persuaded the tribe to donate the pole. See Robin Ridington, "Omaha Survival: A Vanishing Indian Tribe that Would Not Vanish," *American Indian Quarterly* 11 (1987): 37–38.

27. William Least Heat-Moon, *PrairyErth: A Deep Map* (Boston: Houghton Mifflin, 1991), 329. Least Heat-Moon is mistaken about the particulars of the act. See instead Richard B. Morris, *Encyclopedia of American History* (New York: Harper and Brothers, 1953), 439.

28. *Gifford v. Yarborough*, 5 Bing. 163, 130 Eng. Rep. 1023, 1024 (1828).

29. *Jefferis v. East Omaha Land Co.*, 134 U.S. 178, 191 (1890).

30. For an early example of the recognition of this dilemma, see Comment, "Real Property—Navigable Rivers—Accretion to Riparian Land," *Iowa Law Review* 45 (1960): 945–954.

31. Robert E. Beck, "The Wandering Missouri River: A Study in Accretion Law," *North Dakota Law Review* 43 (1967): 449.

32. For a discussion of these legal rules as they pertained to Blackbird Bend, see Laurie Smith Camp, "Land Accretion and Avulsion: The Battle of Blackbird Bend," *Nebraska Law Review* 56 (1977): 814 835. A more general discussion can be found in Paul Jackson, "Alluvio and the Common Law," *Law Quarterly Review* 99 (1983): 412–431.

33. See Ros Jensen, "Blackbird Bend: Landmark Victory in Land Dispute," *Christian Century* 95 (1978): 607.

34. Quoted in *Almanac of the Federal Judiciary* (Washington, D.C.: Prentice Hall, 1992), 1:47.

35. Quoted in "The Tribal Position," *SCJ*, Apr. 30, 1978.

36. Opposition to Final Judgment, attached Memorandum of Points and Authorities, Sept. 12, 1974, no. 790, pp. 5–6, CP1.

37. The quotations and discussion of the trial that follow are based on Trial Transcript, Nov. 1–Dec. 6, 1976, pp. 645, 958, 1987, 1989, 2017, 2095, 2102, 2134, 2358, 2419, 2424, CP1.

38. The best description of this process is in Luna B. Leopold, *Water: A Primer* (San Francisco: W. H. Freeman, 1974), 81–89.

39. Leonard Shengold, *Soul Murder: The Effects of Childhood Abuse and Deprivation* (New Haven: Yale Univ. Press, 1989), 284.

40. *United States v. Wilson*, 433 F. Supp. 67, 72 (N.D. Iowa 1977). Also see, *United States v. Wilson*, 433 F. Supp. 57 (N.D. Iowa 1977), which rules on the important choice of law issues involved in the case.

41. 433 F. Supp. at 78, 84.

42. Quoted in "Principals React Strongly to Indian–White Land Ruling," *DMR*, May 5, 1977.

43. "Indians Balk at Third Notice to Vacate Land," *DMR*, May 13, 1977.

44. "Tribe Gets Temporary Stay on Monona Land," *SCJ*, May 14, 1977.

45. *Omaha Indian Tribe v. Wilson*, 575 F.2d 620 (8th Cir. 1978).

46. The law is 25 U.S.C. § 194 (1834).

47. The quoted material is from 572 F.2d at 631, 638, 649.

48. This is the entire legal history of the consolidated case: *United States* v. *Wilson*, 433 F. Supp. 67 (N.D. Iowa 1977); *Omaha Indian Tribe* v. *Wilson*, 575 F.2d 620 (8th Cir. 1978), *vacated and remanded*, 442 U.S. 653 (1979); *Omaha Indian Tribe, Treaty of 1854 with the United States* v. *Wilson*, 614 F.2d 1153 (8th Cir.), *cert. denied*, 449 U.S. 825 (1980); *United States* v. *Wilson*, 523 F. Supp. 874 (N.D. Iowa 1981); *United States* v. *Wilson*, 707 F.2d 304 (8th Cir. 1982), *cert. denied*, 465 U.S. 1025 (1984); *United States* v. *Wilson*, 578 F. Supp. 1191 (N.D. Iowa 1984), *aff'd in part and rev'd in part*, *Omaha Indian Tribe* v. *Jackson*, 854 F.2d 1089 (8th Cir. 1988), *cert. denied* 490 U.S. 1090 (1989); *United States* v. *Wilson*, 926 F.2d 725 (8th Cir. 1991).

49. Quoted in "Indians, Landowners Gird for Land Battle," *DMR*, Oct. 12, 1980.

50. Quoted in "Iowa Land Belongs to Indians: Court," *DMR*, Apr. 12, 1978.

51. Quoted in "Onawa, Casino Combine Promotion Efforts," *SCJ*, Mar. 7, 1992.

52. Quoted in "For Onawa, New Casino Is an Unwanted Gamble," *DMR*, Jan. 5, 1992.

53. Jeremy Waldron, *The Right to Private Property* (Oxford: Clarendon Press, 1988), 38.

54. Of course, Blackbird Bend is hardly the only piece of land in the world that presents complications for property ownership. Readers might be interested to know of an unusual New Guinea case involving Vulcan Island. The island was formed in a volcanic eruption that took place in 1878. About sixty years later, a second eruption caused the island to disappear and emerge in a slightly different spot. In the 1950s, the Australian Administration asserted its title to the land against a group of native people, the Tolai. The task of sorting out title to the land was further complicated by the fact that the Japanese, who invaded Vulcan Island in 1942, burned the land register set up by the Australian government. See A. W. B. Simpson, "Real Property," in *Annual Survey of Commonwealth Law 1971*, ed. H. W. R. Wade and Harold L. Cryer (London: Butterworths, 1972), 212–216. Also see *Tolain* v. *Administration of the Territory of Papua and New Guinea* [1965–1966], P. & N.G.L.R. 232.

55. "River Complicates Indian Casino Plans," *SCJ*, June 17, 1991.

2. IDENTITY CRISIS IN BAYOU COUNTRY

1. For an update on its history, see John McPhee, *The Control of Nature* (New York: Farrar Straus Giroux, 1989).

2. Harold N. Fisk, *Geological Investigation of the Atchafalaya Basin and the Problem of Mississippi River Diversion*, 2 vols. (Vicksburg: U.S. Army Corps of Engineers, 1952), 1:65–66, 67.

3. Malcolm L. Comeaux, "The Atchafalaya River Raft," *Louisiana Studies* 9 (1970): 217–218; Rodney A. Latimer and Charles W. Schweizer, *The Atchafalaya River Study . . .* 3 vols. (Vicksburg: Mississippi River Commission, 1951), 1:10, C1. The channel changes are referred to as Shreve's Cutoff and were made by Henry M. Shreve, a riverboat captain, to improve navigation on the lower Red River.

4. Pete Daniel, *Deep'n as It Come: The 1927 Mississippi River Flood* (New York: Oxford Univ. Press, 1977), 10.

5. Fisk, *Atchafalaya Basin*, 135, 140–141.

6. Ibid., 80; Frank C. Wells and Charles R. Demas, *Hydrology and Water Quality of the Atchafalaya River Basin* (Baton Rouge: Louisiana Department of Transportation and Development, 1977), 12.

7. Quoted in Jack Rudloe and Anne Rudloe, "Trouble in Bayou Country," *National Geographic*, Sept. 1979, 390. Also see the excellent compilation of maps that shows the changing shape of Grand and Six Mile lakes between 1917 and 1972 in Sherwood M. Gagliano and Johannes L. van Beek, *Environmental Base and Management Study, Atchafalaya Basin, Louisiana* (Washington, D.C.: U.S. Environmental Protection Agency, 1975), 15–19.

8. On the logging of red cypress in the Atchafalaya basin, see D. Gail Abbey, *Life in the Atchafalaya Swamp* (Lafayette, La.: Lafayette Natural History Museum, 1979), 9–12. For an excellent discussion of the settlement history of the Atchafalaya basin, see Malcolm L. Comeaux, *Atchafalaya Swamp Life: Settlement and Folk Occupations*, Geoscience and Man, ed. Bob F. Perkins, vol. 2 (Baton Rouge: Distributed by the School of Geoscience, Louisiana State Univ., 1972).

9. La. Civil Code art. 509 (1870).

10. Under the equal footing doctrine, land beneath navigable waters belongs to the individual states. See M. Thomas Arceneaux, "The Lake Dilemma," *Louisiana Law Review* 35 (1974): 199–200.

11. That battle is surveyed in Martin Reuss, "Along the Atchafalaya: The Challenge of a Vital Resource," *Environment* 30 (May 1988): 6–11, 36–44, and his "Engineers, Science, and the Public Interest: Water Resources Planning in the Atchafalaya Basin," *Journal of Policy History* 3 (1991): 282–308.

12. Roland Barthes, *The Semiotic Challenge*, trans. Richard Howard (New York: Hill and Wang, 1988), 47.

13. *State* v. *Cockrell*, 162 So.2d 361 (La. Ct. App. 1st Cir.), *cert. denied*, 246 La. 343, 164 So.2d 350 (1964).

14. The quotations and discussion of the trial that follow are based on

Trial Transcript, Mar. 7–11, 1960, vol. 882: 116, 118, 132, 140–141, 268–269, 403, 415, 522–523, CP2.

15. "Reasons for Judgment," Aug. 30, 1962, vol. 879: 113, CP2.

16. Ibid., 121.

17. "Reply Brief on Behalf of the State of Louisiana and Gulf Oil Corporation, Plaintiffs–Appellants, in Answer to Brief Filed by Defendants–Appellees," Nov. 22, 1963, vol. 879: 9, 18, CP2.

18. *State v. Erwin*, 173 La. 507, 138 So. 84, 86 (1931).

19. *Miami Corp. v. State*, 186 La. 784, 173 So. 315 (1936), decided five years later, overruled *Erwin* on another issue but "gave tacit approval to the methodology and result in *Erwin*." See Warren M. Schultz, Jr., "Property—Classifying Bodies of Water as Lakes or Streams," *Tulane Law Review* 49 (1974): 210.

20. *Amerada Petroleum Corp. v. State Mineral Board*, 203 La. 473, 14 So.2d 61, 69 (1943).

21. *Amerada Petroleum Corp. v. Case*, 210 La. 630, 27 So.2d 431 (1946). Fifteen years before the *Cockrell* trial, Steinmayer was called to the stand in *Second Amerada*. A man who had spent a good deal of time pondering Louisiana's waterscape, Steinmayer found little but streams there, Arm of Grand Lake included. The trial judge agreed that Arm of Grand Lake was a stream and the supreme court later affirmed this decision.

22. 162 So.2d at 373. "Six Mile Lake," the opinion reads, "is a stream as distinguished from a lake considering it is shown to be a body of water containing currents of sufficient velocity to carry alluvial materials."

23. William Darby, *A Geographical Description of the State of Louisiana* . . . (Philadelphia: John Melish, 1816), 60. Also see 162 So.2d at 370.

24. Walter Prichard, Fred B. Kniffen, and Clair A. Brown, eds., "Southern Louisiana and Southern Alabama in 1819: The Journal of James Leander Cathcart," *Louisiana Historical Quarterly* 28 (1945): 783. According to the court of appeal, these historical sources demonstrated in another way that the body of water in question was indeed a stream. The plaintiffs (appellants) had argued from nineteenth-century maps that the Atchafalaya River actually flowed east of, not through, Lake Chetimaches (Grand Lake). Darby's map, for example, showed this to be the case. But the court of appeal used Darby's and Cathcart's journals to show that in fact the presence of a current and a channel in Grand Lake proved that the Atchafalaya River really did flow directly through Grand and Six Mile lakes, despite what the maps showed. See 162 So.2d at 371.

25. Cathcart also referred to Lake Chetimaches as Grand Lake and Lake Sale.

26. It is, however, worth noting that an effort was made between 1964 and 1970 in the legislature to pass a bill that would have rendered the Louisiana

statutes pertaining to accretion and reliction void in the Atchafalaya basin. Six such efforts were mounted but none of them succeeded.

27. 162 So.2d at 381–382, 384. Herget also interpreted the decision in *Second Amerada* to imply that Grand Lake was in fact a lake. See ibid., 383.

28. Michel Foucault, *The Order of Things: An Archaeology of the Human Sciences* (1970; reprint, New York: Vintage Books, 1973), xvii.

29. *State* v. *Placid Oil Co.*, 300 So.2d 154 (La. 1974).

30. See "Reasons for Judgment," Sept. 24, 1970, vol. 1980, pt. 5: 1798–1852. The discussion that follows is based on Trial Transcript, Apr. 17–20, 1967, vol. 1980, pt. 4: 695, 696, 702, 704, 706, 720–746, 748–750, 767–771, 802, 1025–1028, 1058–1059, 1070, 1075, 1081–1083, 1086, 1091–1092, CP3.

31. "Calcasieu River," Kolb pointed out, "flows into Calcasieu Lake during flood flow at 180,000 cubic feet per second." Yet everyone, including Steinmayer, agreed that Louisiana's Calcasieu Lake was truly a lake. Indeed, Steinmayer admitted this under cross-examination in the *Cockrell* trial. See Trial Transcript, Mar. 7–11, 1960, 161, CP2.

32. "Reasons for Judgment," Sept. 24, 1970, pp. 1824, 1826, CP3.

33. *State* v. *Placid Oil Co.*, 274 So.2d 402, 414–417 (La. Ct. App. 1st Cir. 1973).

34. Judge Tucker, although he concurred with the majority opinion, urged a return to the law established in *Erwin*.

35. 274 So.2d at 432. Landry distinguished the *First Amerada* case, which the majority saw as having overruled *Erwin sub silentio*, because it had involved a much smaller body of water than Grand- Six Mile Lake. The *Cockrell* decision, which of course concerned the same body of water at issue here, he now regarded as wrong, despite what he had said back then.

36. "Petition by State of Louisiana, Plaintiff–Appellant, for Writ of Certiorari or Review to Reverse and Set Aside Decision of Court of Appeal, First Circuit, Rendered December 26, 1972," n.d., 33, CP4.

37. The debate continued to center on the question of meaning. According to Guste, the court of appeal had attached "an arbitrary technical meaning equivalent to 'current'" on the word *stream*. This was contrary, he argued, to the "usual signification" of the word. "The words 'rivers or other streams' in Article 509 are not words of art," he wrote, "but unambiguous words of popular use." Instead, the court had chosen to adopt Steinmayer's sense of what constituted a stream, hardly the usual meaning given to the word. The natural world according to Steinmayer was one in which the word *stream* had a meaning that was overwhelmingly geological, rooted in the science that he had practiced for most of his life. "Lay and expert testimony is," as Guste admitted, "of course, relevant to establish facts that may be pertinent for the formulation of a legal opinion. But this does not mean that classification is a factual determination.

What may be defined as a lake in the field of geology may be a stream under Article 509, and *vice versa.*" See ibid., 24–25, 30.

On this last point, both sides in the case agreed. According to lawyers for Texaco, which had intervened on the defendants' side, the supreme court "is concerned only with the characteristics of the water body as will bring it either within or without the purview of the above articles of the Code, and not its classification by cartographers or in the science of geology." Nevertheless, in Texaco's view, Steinmayer had offered an interpretation of *stream* that fell within the meaning established by Louisiana legal precedent. Kolb's standards for defining a lake "may be meaningful in the field of Geology," wrote Texaco, "but obviously have no bearing in determining the classification of a water body for the limited purposes of Civil Code Articles 509 and 510." See "Original Brief on the Merits on Behalf of Texaco," Sept. 20, 1973, 27, 51, CP4.

38. 300 So.2d at 159.

39. Ibid., 167, 170.

40. "Brief of Defendants–Appellees on Rehearing," Apr. 29, 1974, 18, CP4.

41. "Old Grand Lake Land Is 'Refuge,'" *Times-Picayune* (New Orleans), May 10, 1974.

42. 300 So.2d at 173, 175. Justice Summers chose to dissent from the opinion and explained why on pp. 178–180.

43. Joe W. Sanders, "The Anatomy of Proof in Civil Actions," *Louisiana Law Review* 28 (1968): 297.

44. On this issue, see Clifford Geertz, *Local Knowledge: Further Essays in Interpretive Anthropology* (New York: Basic Books, 1983), 173.

45. Quoted in "State Declared Owner of Oil-Rich Lands," *Times-Picayune* (New Orleans), June 11, 1974.

46. "Brief of Defendants in Support of Their Application for Rehearing," July 22, 1974, 15–17, CP4. Bodies of water are not the only element of the natural world to present problems for legal classification. It may interest readers to know of a famous U.S. Supreme Court case that dealt with whether a tomato was a fruit or a vegetable. The issue was raised because of a tariff provision that taxed fruits and vegetables differently. The court held that a tomato is a vegetable because that is the common understanding. "Botanically speaking," wrote the court, "tomatoes are the fruit of a vine, just as are cucumbers, squashes, beans, and peas. But in the common language of the people, whether sellers or consumers of provisions, all these are vegetables, which are grown in kitchen gardens, and which, whether eaten cooked or raw, are, like potatoes, carrots, parsnips, turnips, beets, cauliflower, cabbage, celery and lettuce, usually served at dinner in, with or after the soup, fish or meats which constitute the principal part of the repast, and not, like fruits generally, as dessert." See *Nix* v. *Hedden*, 149 U.S. 304, 307 (1892).

47. Tzvetan Todorov, *Theories of the Symbol*, trans. Catherine Porter (Ithaca: Cornell Univ. Press, 1982), 243.

48. Walker Percy, *The Message in the Bottle: How Queer Man Is, How Queer Language Is, and What One Has to Do with the Other* (New York: Farrar, Straus and Giroux, 1975), 34–35.

49. Ibid., 261.

50. Recently, near Lake Providence, Louisiana, a similar dispute over property and names has emerged. This time the conflict involves the states of Louisiana and Mississippi, which are battling over who owns Stack Island, a tiny piece of land in the Mississippi River. Mississippi argues that the river moved the island but that it still falls within the state's legal boundary. Louisiana, however, says that Stack Island no longer exists. What people now call Stack Island is just sediment from up the river, sediment that Louisiana argues it is entitled to. Said one supporter of this position, "A lifetime of experience tells me that Stack Island is gone and this bit of land is not Stack Island. . . . What's in a name? It doesn't make an elephant a dog." A judge ruled in favor of Mississippi in 1989. The decision was later reversed and is now pending before the U.S. Supreme Court. Quoted material is from "'Tiny Island in a Stream Is in Court," *NYT*, Dec. 14, 1992.

51. Susanne K. Langer, *Philosophy in a New Key: A Study in the Symbolism of Reason, Rite, and Art* (Cambridge: Harvard Univ. Press, 1960), 142.

52. Robert Darnton, *The Great Cat Massacre and Other Episodes in French Cultural History* (1984; reprint, New York: Vintage Books, 1985), 192.

3. NOTES FROM UNDERGROUND:

THE PRIVATE LIFE OF WATER

1. Dean E. Mann, "Law and Politics of Groundwater in Arizona," *Arizona Law Review* 2 (1960): 243.

2. Samuel F. Turner, "Ground-Water Resources of the Salt River Valley Water Users Association" (Arizona State Library, Phoenix, Sept. 22, 1952, typescript), 8.

3. Donald Worster, *Rivers of Empire: Water, Aridity and the Growth of the American West* (New York: Pantheon, 1985), 172.

4. Fyodor Dostoevsky, *Notes from Underground and The Grand Inquisitor*, trans. Ralph E. Matlaw (New York: E. P. Dutton and Co., 1960), 29.

5. Underground Water Commission, *The Underground Water Resources of Arizona*, 20th Ariz. Legislature, 2d sess., Jan. 1, 1953, 69, 71t.

6. "Pumping Threat Is Dust Bowl," *Arizona Republic*, May 29, 1946.

7. U.S. Department of Commerce, Weather Bureau, *Climatological*

Data: Arizona, Annual Summary 1950 (San Francisco: U.S. Department of Commerce, Weather Bureau, 1951), 182.

8. "A Decade of Drought Cracks Arizona," *Life*, Aug. 13, 1951, 19.

9. Underground Water Commission, *Underground Water*, 66t.

10. G. E. P. Smith, "The Groundwater Supply of the Eloy District in Pinal County, Arizona," University of Arizona, Agricultural Experiment Station, *Technical Bulletin*, no. 87 (June 1940): 15–16.

11. Goree recalled their conversation at a senate hearing. See Senate Appropriations Committee, Hearings on S.B. 56 and S.B. 66, 20th Ariz. Legislature, 2d sess., Feb. 18, 1952, 66.

12. S. F. Turner and R. L. Cushman, "Pumpage and Ground-water Levels in Arizona in 1950" (U.S. Department of Interior, Geological Survey, Tucson, 1950), 9.

13. Dostoevsky, *Notes from Underground*, 29.

14. Mann, "Groundwater in Arizona," 243.

15. G. E. P. Smith to J. Byron McCormick, Feb. 12, 1953, Arizona State Library, Phoenix, 5.

16. Robert G. Dunbar, "The Arizona Groundwater Controversy at Mid-Century," *Arizona and the West* 19 (1977): 11–12.

17. Mann, "Groundwater in Arizona," 249.

18. 1948 Ariz. Sess. Laws, 6th spec. sess., chap. 5.

19. Hearings on S.B. 56 and S.B. 66, 106–107.

20. Senate Committee on Judiciary and Committee on Agriculture and Irrigation, Hearings on Senate Bill no. 1, 18th Ariz. Legislature, 4th spec. sess., Jan. 29, 1948, 91.

21. Ibid.

22. Public Hearing on House Bill no. 8, House of Representatives, 18th Ariz. Legislature, Jan. 30, 1947, 61, 65.

23. Ibid., 16.

24. The biographical information is from Betty Kruse Accomazzo, *Laveen Centennial History, 1884–1984* (Laveen, Ariz.: Laveen Community Council, 1984), 20; "Can You Pump Your Neighbor Dry?" *Business Week*, Aug. 16, 1952, 79.

25. "Pump Your Neighbor Dry?" 78–79.

26. See the complaint and briefs in *Bristor* v. *Cheatham*, 73 Ariz. 228, 240 P.2d 185 (1952) (microfilm, State of Arizona Department of Library, Archives and Public Records, 5334).

27. *Howard* v. *Perrin*, 8 Ariz. 347, 76 P. 460 (1905), *aff'd*, 200 U.S. 71 (1906).

28. *Maricopa County Mun. Water Conservation Dist. No. 1* v. *Southwest Cotton Co.*, 39 Ariz. 65, 4 P.2d 369, 374 (1931).

29. John D. Leshy and James Belanger, "Arizona Law Where Ground and Surface Water Meet," *Arizona State Law Journal* 20 (1988): 679.

30. 240 P.2d at 188, 189. The court's decision in the case was heavily influenced by the thoughts of retired Justice Alfred Lockwood. Lockwood had written many of the important water decisions in the state including the decision in *Southwest Cotton* (1931). According to one report, the court solicited Lockwood's view in the *Bristor* case. Lockwood issued an advisory opinion just before he died on October 29, 1951, which urged the court to reverse its position on underground water. "The common law of England," he wrote, "is only binding so far as it is consistent with and adapted to the natural and physical conditions of the territory and the necessities of the people thereof. I think that the common law regarding percolating water is clearly inapplicable to the local conditions and necessities of the people of Arizona." Quoted in "High Court Water Edict Approved by Lockwood," *Arizona Republic*, Jan. 24, 1952.

31. William Blackstone, *Commentaries on the Laws of England*, 1st ed. (1765–1769; reprint, Chicago: Univ. of Chicago Press, 1979), 2:18.

32. Quoted in "Water Code Foes Open Fight at Casa Grande," *Arizona Republic*, Jan. 10, 1952. According to the newspaper, "Ironside said that since the establishment of government in Arizona groundwater has been owned—just like a house—by the owner of the land."

33. The group was originally formed to fight child labor laws.

34. Quoted in "Angry Farmers Protest Court's Water Decision," *Arizona Republic*, Jan. 16, 1952.

35. *Bristor v. Cheatham*, 75 Ariz. 227, 255 P.2d 173, 176 (1953).

36. Dostoevsky, *Notes from Underground*, 29–30.

37. Marshall Berman, *All That Is Solid Melts into Air: The Experience of Modernity* (1982; reprint, New York: Penguin Books, 1988), 243. Emphasis is mine.

4. CLOUDBUSTING IN FULTON COUNTY

1. See, e.g., Clark C. Spence, *The Rainmakers: American 'Pluviculture' to World War II* (Lincoln: Univ. of Nebraska Press, 1980), and William B. Meyer, "The Life and Times of U.S. Weather: What Can We Do About It?" *American Heritage* 37 (June/July 1986): 38–48.

2. Quoted in C. Lester Walker, "The Man Who Makes Weather," *Harper's*, Jan. 1950, 67.

3. "Nick the Rain Maker," *Life*, Sept. 8, 1947, 53–56; also see, "Man-Made Snowstorm," *Life*, Dec. 30, 1946, 52–54.

4. Ralph E. Huschke, "A Brief History of Weather Modification Since 1946," *Bulletin of the American Meteorological Society* 44 (July 1963): 428.

5. Pennsylvania Crop Reporting Service, *Pennsylvania Crops and Livestock: Annual Summary 1960* (Harrisburg: Pennsylvania Crop Reporting Service, 1960), 75, 87.

6. Jerome Namias, "Nature and Possible Causes of the Northeastern United States Drought During 1962–65," *Monthly Weather Review* 94 (Sept. 1966): 543–554.

7. *American Men and Women of Science: A Biographical Directory of Today's Leaders in Physical, Biological and Related Sciences*, 17th ed. (New York: Bowker, 1989), 3:863; Senate Committee on Commerce, Hearings on S. 23 and S. 2916, pt. 1, 89th Cong., 1st and 2d sess., Nov. 5, 10, 1965; Feb. 21, 24, 25 and Mar. 7, 8, 1966, 248, 265.

8. Wallace E. Howell, "Cloud Seeding and the Law in the Blue Ridge Area," *Bulletin of the American Meteorological Society* 46 (June 1965): 328.

9. "Hail Hits County Wednesday Evening," *Mercersburg Journal* (Penn.), July 1, 1960; "Hail Damages Fruit in 75% of Major County Orchards," *Mercersburg Journal*, July 27, 1962.

10. Quoted in "Battle of the Clouds," *Time*, Aug. 31, 1962, 16.

11. Quoted in "Hail Control Meeting Attended by Many Farmers," *Mercersburg Journal*, June 22, 1962.

12. For more on weather cultures, see Andrew Ross, *Strange Weather: Culture, Science and Technology in the Age of Limits* (London: Verso, 1991), 214–249.

13. "War to Win the Weather," Letter to the Editor, *FD*, Oct. 8, 1964.

14. Editorial, *FD*, July 30, 1964.

15. "Co. Commissioner Hits Cloud Seeding," Letter to the Editor, *FCN*, Sept. 24, 1964.

16. Editorial, *FD*, Sept. 10, 1964.

17. "Statement by the Penna. Natural Weather Association," *Mercersburg Journal*, Jan. 1, 1965.

18. "The Bible Knows," *FCN*, Oct. 1, 1964. I Kings 8:35–36 reads, "When heaven is shut up and there is no rain because they have sinned against thee, if they pray toward this place, and acknowledge thy name, and turn from their sin, when thou dost afflict them, then hear thou in heaven, and forgive the sin of thy servants, thy people Israel, when thou dost teach them the good way in which they should walk; and grant rain upon thy land, which thou hast given to thy people as an inheritance." II Chronicles 7:13–14 reads, "When I shut up the heavens so that there is no rain, or command the locust to devour the land, or send pestilence among my people, if my people who are called by my name humble themselves, and pray and seek my face, and turn from their

wicked ways, then I will hear from heaven, and will forgive their sin and heal their land." Amos 4:7–11 reads in part, "'And I also withheld the rain from you when there were yet three months to the harvest; I would send rain upon one city, and send no rain upon another city; one field would be rained upon, and the field on which it did not rain withered; so two or three cities wandered to one city to drink water, and were not satisfied; yet you did not return to me,' says the Lord." See the *New Oxford Annotated Bible with the Apocrypha*, ed. Herbert G. May and Bruce M. Metzger (New York: Oxford Univ. Press, 1977).

19. Quoted in "Weather Ass'n. Gets Public Support," *FD*, Oct. 1, 1964.

20. *Slutsky* v. *City of New York*, 97 N.Y.S. 2d 238, 239 (Sup. Ct. 1950).

21. Edward Coke, *The First Part of the Institutes of the Lawes of England* . . . (London, 1628), 4a.

22. If the old common law had nothing to say on weather, it did have a little to offer on the topic of wind (i.e., when people built houses that obstructed the wind near a windmill). See Michael Bowles, *Gale on Easements*, 13th ed. (London: Sweet and Maxwell, 1959), 237–239.

23. However, readers might be interested to know about a case involving a Tasmanian cat. The defendant in the matter fired a rifle at the cat, which had crossed onto his property but at the time it was killed had fled onto a shed located on the plaintiff's adjoining land. The plaintiff sought damages for the mental distress caused by seeing the death of the pet as well as for trespass to land caused by the bullet. The court held that there could be recovery for trespass, citing the ad coelum maxim. It denied the claim for mental distress. See *Davies* v. *Bennison*, 22 T.L.R. 52 (1927).

24. *Hinman* v. *Pacific Air Transport*, 84 F.2d 755, 757 (C.C.A. 9th Cir., 1936). For more on the ad coelum doctrine, see Howard H. Hackley, "Trespassers in the Sky," *Minnesota Law Review* 21 (1937): 773–804, and Paul Binzak, Richard P. Buellesback, and Irving Zirbel, "Comments: Rights of Private Land Owners as Against Artificial Rain Makers," *Marquette Law Review* 34 (1951): 262–275.

25. Reconciling weather modification and property law preoccupied many legal scholars during the late forties and fifties. See, e.g., "Who Owns the Clouds?" *Stanford Law Review* 1 (1948): 43–63; Alexander L. Bensinger, "From Man-Made Rain, a Flood of Legal Problems," *Temple Law Quarterly* 22 (1948): 99–105; Vaughn C. Ball, "Shaping the Law of Weather Control," *Yale Law Journal* 58 (1949): 213–244; and "Legal Clouds for Rainmakers," *Albany Law Review* 14 (1950): 204–214.

26. See Clinton P. Anderson and Wallace E. Howell, "Should the U.S. Government Control the Rain Makers?" *Rotarian* 78 (Mar. 1951): 9.

27. "West Virginia Legislature Holds Hearing on Cloud-Seeding Bill," *FD*, Feb. 11, 1965; "Two Year Ban on Weather Modification Urged in Md.," *FD*, Mar. 18, 1965; Barbara Leese, "Cloud Seeding: When, Where, How and Why?" *FD*, June 16, 1977.

28. Quoted in "The Cloud Seeding Issue," *FCN*, Sept. 10, 1964.

29. Howell, "Cloud Seeding and the Law," 331.

30. Ibid., 328, 331.

31. Senate Committee on Commerce, Hearings on S. 23 and S. 2916, 252.

32. Edward A. Morris, "The Law and Weather Modification," *Bulletin of the American Meteorological Society* 46 (Oct. 1965): 622.

33. "Governor Vetoes Cloud Seeding Bill," *FCN*, July 29, 1965; Act of Nov. 9, 1965, no. 331, Pa. Laws 677; "Franklin County Becomes First to Ban Weather Tampering," *FD*, Feb. 24, 1966; "Commissioners Ban Weather Modification in Fulton County," *FD*, Mar. 3, 1966.

34. Quoted in "In the Clouds," *Philadelphia Inquirer*, Apr. 18, 1978.

35. The quotations and discussion that follow are based on Trial Transcript, Feb. 2, 1966, 10, 21, 27, 52, 70, 75, 88, 89, 147, 148, 223–226, 302, 372, 389, 402, CP5.

36. See the discussion in "Who Owns the Clouds?" 51–57.

37. Raymond Williams, *Keywords: A Vocabulary of Culture and Society*, rev. ed. (1983; reprint, New York: Oxford Univ. Press, 1985), 219.

38. Defendants' Brief, n.d., 7, CP5.

39. Defendants' Reply Brief, Sept. 8, 1966, 3, CP5.

40. *Pennsylvania Natural Weather Ass'n* v. *Blue Ridge Weather Modification Ass'n*, 44 Pa. D. & C.2d 749, 756–758, 759–760 (C.P. 1968).

41. Ibid., 761–763.

42. On the transformation of nineteenth-century water law, see Morton J. Horwitz, *The Transformation of American Law, 1780–1860* (Cambridge: Harvard Univ. Press, 1977), 31–53; and Theodore Steinberg, *Nature Incorporated: Industrialization and the Waters of New England* (New York: Cambridge Univ. Press, 1991), 140–148.

43. The efficacy of weather modification is still unclear. Some studies suggest that it works, but many more show results that are not valid statistically. See Richard A. Kerr, "Cloud Seeding: One Success in 35 Years," *Science*, Aug. 6, 1982, 519–521; "Cloud Seeding," *Science*, Oct. 29, 1982, 424, 426; and Stanley A. Changnon et al., "Illinois Precipitation Research: A Focus on Cloud and Precipitation Modification," *Bulletin of the American Meteorological Society* 72 (1991): 587–604.

44. Max Horkheimer, *Eclipse of Reason* (New York: Oxford Univ. Press, 1947), 93.

5. THREE-D DEEDS: THE RISE OF
AIR RIGHTS IN NEW YORK

1. Quoted in Talk of the Town, "Tallest," *New Yorker*, Sept. 9, 1967, 38; also see Ernest Flagg, "The Singer Building, New York," *Architects' and Builders' Magazine* 40 (1908): 429–444, for an excellent description of the building.

2. Quoted in "Tallest," 38. On the destruction of the building, also see "End of Skyscraper: Daring in '08, Obscure in '68," *NYT*, Mar. 27, 1968, 49, col. 1.

3. Stephen Zoll, "Superville: New York—Aspects of Very High Bulk," *Massachusetts Review* 14 (1973): 493–494. The building was also called Merrill Lynch Plaza for a time.

4. Karl Marx, "Speech at the Anniversary of the *People's Paper*," in *The Marx-Engels Reader*, ed. Robert C. Tucker, 2d ed. (New York: Norton, 1978), 577.

5. Karl Marx and Friedrich Engels, "Manifesto of the Communist Party," ibid., 476. Also see Marshall Berman's brilliant book, *All That Is Solid Melts into Air: The Experience of Modernity* (1982; reprint, New York: Penguin Books, 1988), which inspired this chapter.

6. He was paraphrasing Edward Coke. William Blackstone, *Commentaries on the Laws of England*, 1st ed. (1765–1769; reprint, Chicago: Univ. of Chicago Press, 1979), 2:17.

7. Ibid., 10. Also see my discussion in chap. 4.

8. However, there did evolve in Britain, at some point, the idea of "horizontal hereditaments," which consisted of a lateral division of space and essentially amounted to title to a bit of airspace. See James Edward Hogg, "The Effect of Tenure on Real Property Law," *Law Quarterly Review* 25 (1909): 184–185.

9. See Robert R. Wright, *The Law of Airspace* (Indianapolis: Bobbs-Merrill, 1968), 36.

10. Quoted in Stuart S. Ball, "The Jural Nature of Land," *Illinois Law Review* 23 (1928): 60n.

11. *Butler v. Frontier Telephone Co.*, 186 N.Y. 486, 79 N.E. 716, 718 (1906).

12. Stuart S. Ball, "The Vertical Extent of Ownership in Land," *University of Pennsylvania Law Review* 76 (1928): 673.

13. Laird Bell, "Air Rights," *Illinois Law Review* 23 (1928): 252.

14. See James J. Brennan, "Lots of Air—A Subdivision in the Sky," *Section of Real Property, Probate and Trust Law* (Proceedings, Aug. 22–24, 1955, American Bar Center, Chicago), 25.

15. Theodore Schmidt, "Public Utility Air Rights," *Report of the Fifty-second Annual Meeting of American Bar Association* (Baltimore: Lord Baltimore Press, 1929), 839, 841. I borrow the term "deterritorialized" from Henri Lefebvre, *The Production of Space*, trans. Donald Nicholson-Smith (Oxford: Basil Blackwell, 1991), 347.

16. William J. Wilgus, "The Grand Central Terminal in Perspective," *Transactions of the American Society of Civil Engineers* 106 (1941): 1003.

17. Carl W. Condit, *The Port of New York: A History of the Rail and Terminal System from the Grand Central Electrification to the Present* (Chicago: Univ. of Chicago Press, 1981), 85, 97–98.

18. Seymour I. Toll, *Zoned American* (New York: Grossman, 1969), 71; Zoll, "Superville," 494.

19. Rem Koolhaas, *Delirious New York: A Retroactive Manifesto for Manhattan* (New York: Oxford Univ. Press, 1978), 13, 15.

20. On the postindustrialization of New York, see John Hull Mollenkopf, "The Postindustrial Transformation of the Political Order in New York City," in *Power, Culture, and Place: Essays on New York City*, ed. John Hull Mollenkopf (New York: Russell Sage, 1988), 225–229; and Matthew Drennan, "The Decline and Rise of the New York Economy," in *Dual City: Restructuring New York*, ed. John H. Mollenkopf and Manuel Castells (New York: Russell Sage, 1991), 25–41.

21. Samuel B. Kuckley, *Rebuilding Manhattan: A Study of New Office Construction* (New York: Real Estate Board of New York, 1972), 10t, 14t.

22. Quote is from Condit, *The Port of New York*, 198; also see pp. 190–198 on the progress of the Grand Central air rights ventures between 1913 and 1932. On the Waldorf wine cellar, see Creighton Peet, "No Land? Then Build it on Air," *Popular Mechanics*, Jan. 1966, 134, 136.

23. Lefebvre, *The Production of Space*, 325, 337.

24. "World's Loftiest Tower May Rise on Site of Grand Central Terminal," *NYT*, Sept. 8, 1954, 1, col. 7.

25. Kuckley, *Rebuilding Manhattan*, 22t, 23t.

26. "Grand Central May Get a Tower," *NYT*, Sept. 21, 1967, 1, col. 4; "Breuer to Design Terminal Tower," *NYT*, Feb. 24, 1968, 30, col. 3; "Grand Central Tower Will Top Pan Am Building," *NYT*, June 20, 1968, 1, col. 4. As far back as 1911, there were plans to put a twenty-three-story office building on top of the terminal. It was never built. See William D. Middleton, *Grand Central: The World's Greatest Railway Terminal* (San Marino, Cal.: Golden West Books, 1977), 136.

27. "Architecture: Grotesquerie Astride a Palace," *NYT*, June 20, 1968, 37, col. 3.

28. Quoted in "New Tower Sought for Grand Central," *NYT*, Apr. 11, 1969, 1, col. 7.

29. Quoted in "Landmarks Panel Bars Office Tower Over Grand Central," *NYT*, Aug. 27, 1969, 1, col. 4.

30. Apparently, the Department of Buildings interpreted the zoning code from the 1920s to 1945 in such a way that builders were able to merge zoning lots and thus gain additional air rights over what the zoning law allowed. The practice ended in 1945, was resumed ten years later, and then stopped in 1959. See "Air Rights Ruling to be Tested Here," *NYT*, Mar. 30, 1958, sec. 8, 1, col. 1, and "Floor Area in New Skyscrapers May be Shrunk by Court Ruling," *NYT*, Jan. 11, 1959, sec. 8, 1, col. 5.

31. "New Zoning Plan Offered to Guide Growth of City," *NYT*, Feb. 16, 1959, 1, col. 8; also see S. J. Makielski, Jr., *The Politics of Zoning: The New York Experience* (New York: Columbia Univ. Press, 1966), 70–106, for a history of postwar efforts to pass a new zoning law in New York.

32. David Alan Richards, "Development Rights Transfer in New York City," *Yale Law Journal* 82 (1972): 338, 344–349.

33. Ibid., 351.

34. On TDRs, see the following works by John J. Costonis: "Development-Rights Transfer: A Proposal for Financing Landmarks Preservation," *Real Estate Law Journal* 1 (1972): 163–174; "Whichever Way You Slice It, DRT Is Here to Stay," *Planning* 40 (July 1974): 10–15; and *Space Adrift: Landmark Preservation and the Marketplace* (Urbana: Univ. of Illinois Press, 1974).

35. In 1968, the New York Central Railroad and Pennsylvania Railroad merged to form the Pennsylvania New York Central Transportation Company, better known as Penn Central.

36. Quoted in Richards, "Development Rights Transfer," 356; also see his discussion of the amendment on 353–358.

37. Quoted in Eleanore Carruth, "Manhattan's Office Building Binge," *Fortune*, Oct. 1969, 115.

38. *Penn Central Transportation Co.* v. *City of New York*, 438 U.S. 104, 130–131 (1978). It was a six-to-three decision, with Justice Rehnquist writing the dissenting opinion.

39. 438 U.S. at 137. For an analysis of the opinion that advocates that the supreme court adopt a more modern concept of property (in keeping with the need to buy and sell air freely), see Mary B. Spector, "Vertical and Horizontal Aspects of Takings Jurisprudence: Is Airspace Property?" *Cardozo Law Review* 7 (1986): 489, 510–518. Also see Norman Marcus, "The Grand Slam Grand Central Terminal Decision: A *Euclid* for Landmarks, Favorable Notice for TDR and a Resolution of the Regulatory/Taking Impasse," *Ecology Law Quarterly* 7 (1978): 731–752.

40. Quotes are from "Tower Over Grand Central Barred as Court Upholds Landmarks Law," *NYT*, June 27, 1978, 1, col. 1. The subsequent history of the terminal's vast reserve of unused air rights is as follows: Philip Morris

had already bought—in the late seventies—75,000 square feet for the construction of a new building at Park and Forty-second Street. Then, in the following decade, a real estate partnership owned by Wall Street's First Boston Company negotiated a deal for 1.5 million square feet, the biggest air rights sale in history. First Boston planned to use about half of those rights to build a skyscraper at 383 Madison Avenue, a seventy-four-story tower to replace a much shorter (14-story) office building dating from 1923. The tower was never built. A dispute surfaced over whether Penn Central could legally transfer its terminal air rights to the tower site. Under the zoning rules, such a transfer had to follow a contiguous chain of landownership. Back in the seventies when the railroad was facing bankruptcy, it had sold a large number of properties in the Grand Central area. Still, the railroad argued that it retained title to the *subsurface* lots, allowing it to transfer the air rights from the terminal up to Madison and Forty-sixth Street, the site of the new tower. The City Planning Commission ruled against the railroad in 1989. By selling its property, the commission explained, the company had broken the chain of title necessary to transfer the unused air rights. Sylvia Deutsch, chairperson of the planning commission, explained that approving the sale would have far-ranging consequences. "One could establish a link or a chain going past Yonkers, conceivably," she remarked. "If you establish the principle that a subsurface lot qualifies as a zoning lot, then one could establish chains that would travel in many directions. Certainly, all the way up Park Avenue." The decision was recently upheld by the New York Supreme Court. See "Panel Rejects Plan to Shift Grand Central's Air Rights," *NYT*, Aug. 24, 1989, sec. 2, 3, col. 5. Also see, "Plan for Tower Uses Air Rights of Rail Station," *NYT*, Sept. 17, 1986, sec. 2, 1, col. 4, and "A Battle Looms Over Grand Central's Air Space," *NYT*, July 6, 1989, sec. 2, 3, col. 2.

Most recently, the terminal's reserve of air rights has interfered with the restoration of the deteriorating physical condition of the terminal itself. The Cincinnati-based Penn Central Corporation, which owns the terminal and its air rights, has been leasing the terminal to the Metropolitan Transportation Authority (MTA), which in turn allows its subsidiary, Metro-North, to operate the terminal. But the MTA has only reluctantly carried out restoring the declining terminal since any improvements made ultimately would redound to the financial advantage of the building's owner, i.e., Penn Central. Also, the MTA has shied away from buying the terminal itself because the building's enormously lucrative store of air rights would add tens of millions of dollars to the asking price of the building. So there has been pressure on the City Planning Department to come up with a zoning plan that would allow Penn Central to capitalize on its air rights. In an official statement made in 1992, Penn Central said, "The city and community should not misunderstand Penn Central's resolve, and that is to realize the value of the air rights, which value has been denied it for so long." (Quoted in "Grand Central Owner Seeks Broader Use of Air Rights," *NYT*, May 3, 1992, sec. 10, 1, col. 5.) Special zoning options that would help Penn Central find a place for its air rights have since been proposed by both the corporation and city planners. But as of December 1993, Penn Central and the MTA were getting ready to sign a new long-term lease that would give the MTA effective control of the building and forbid Penn Central from developing the airspace over the landmark. The new lease will allow the MTA to push ahead with its planned renovations. Still, however, even under the terms of the new lease, Penn Central will retain ownership over the terminal's unused air rights. See "Transit Agency Seeking to Buy Grand Central," *NYT*, Aug. 30, 1990, sec. 2, 1, col. 5, and "Deal Reached on Restoration of Grand Central Terminal," *NYT*, Dec. 21, 1993, 1, col. 1.

41. Quoted in "Planners Seek to Shift Custom House Air Rights," *NYT*, Apr. 9, 1970, sec. 8, 56, col. 4.

42. They included Amster Yard, the Villard Houses, the Philip Morris Building, and the Continental Center.

43. David Alan Richards, "Transferable Development Rights: Corrective, Catastrophe, or Curiosity," *Real Estate Law Journal* 12 (1983): 26, 43–48. The zoning law was amended in 1977, Richards notes, to "facilitate the private sector transfer process." On the zoning law change, see Terrence Kennedy, "New York City Zoning Resolution Section 12–10: A Third Phase in the Evolution of Airspace Law," *Fordham Urban Law Journal* 11 (1983): 1039–1056.

44. Lefebvre, *The Production of Space*, 338.

45. All quotes below are from C. Ray Smith, "Squaring Off on Park Avenue: A Gentlemen's Club K.O.'s the Real-Estate Kings," *New York*, Nov. 27, 1978, 47–52.

46. Koolhaas, *Delirious New York*, 126.

47. John Bartlett, *Familiar Quotations: A Collection of Passages, Phrases, and Proverbs Traced to Their Sources in Ancient and Modern Literature*, ed. Justin Kaplan, 16th ed. (Boston: Little, Brown and Co., 1992), 370.

48. Quoted in Sy Rubin and Jonathan Mandell, *Trump Tower* (Secaucus, N.J.: Lyle Stuart, 1984), 9.

49. Donald J. Trump with Tony Schwartz, *Trump: The Art of the Deal* (1987; reprint, New York: Warner Books, 1989), 163.

50. "If you want sunlight, move to Kansas" is what Der Scutt told one tower opponent. Quoted in Rubin and Mandell, *Trump Tower*, 27.

51. Regarding the city planning commission, Trump explains, "If you want Bonwit to return to Fifth Avenue, I told them, you're going to have to give me my zoning." Trump with Schwartz, *Trump*, 170.

52. Quoted in Trump with Schwartz, *Trump*, 154.

53. Quoted in Rubin and Mandell, *Trump Tower*, 44.

54. David Harvey, *The Urban Experience* (Baltimore: Johns Hopkins Univ. Press, 1989), 177.

55. "Trading Air to Build Towers," *NYT*, Feb. 21, 1986, sec. 4, 1, col. 3.

56. Quoted in "Trading Air to Build Towers."

57. I borrow here from Marc Reisner who uses the term "cash-register dams." See Marc Reisner, *Cadillac Desert: The American West and Its Disappearing Water* (1986; reprint, New York: Penguin Books, 1987).

58. Quoted in "$1 Million Air Sale Proves Godsend to Church," *NYT*, May 3, 1982, sec. 2, 3, col. 3.

59. Quotes are from "Battle of St. Bart's Goes to Landmarks Panel," *NYT*, Feb. 1, 1984, sec. 2, 1, col. 3.

60. Quoted in "Court Ends Tower Plan at St. Bart's," *NYT*, Mar. 5, 1991, sec. 2, 1, col. 6. On the design of the second tower, see "A Smaller Office Tower Is Planned by St. Bart's," *NYT*, Dec. 21, 1984, sec. 2, 3, col. 5.

61. Lefebvre, *The Production of Space*, 338.

PAPER MOON: A CONCLUSION

1. Robert A. Heinlein, *The Man Who Sold the Moon: Harriman and the Escape from Earth to the Moon!* 3d ed. (Chicago: Shasta Publishers, 1953), 173, 194. The reference is to Pope Alexander VI's famous Papal Bull of 1493, which divided up the New World between Spain and Portugal. See Kenneth Anderson Finch, "Territorial Claims to Celestial Bodies," in Senate Committee on Aeronautical and Space Sciences, *Legal Problems of Space Exploration: A Symposium*, 87th Cong., 1st sess., 1961, S. Doc. 26, 628.

2. Heinlein, *Man Who Sold the Moon*, 182–184.

3. "Robert Coles Files Claim on Moon," *Glen Cove Record Pilot*, Nov. 17, 1955; quote is from the quitclaim deed that Coles offered investors.

4. Quoted in "Moon Is on Sale, Only $1 an Acre," *NYT*, Nov. 22, 1955, 37, col. 6.

5. Quoted in "For Sale: Plots Out of this World," *Newsday*, Nov. 16, 1955.

6. Quotes are from "Down-to-Earth Probers Blue over Moon Sale," *Newsday*, Nov. 23, 1955.

7. Quoted in "'Moon Over Miami' Eclipses LI Claim," *Newsday*, Nov. 25, 1955.

8. Oscar Schachter, "Who Owns the Universe?" in *Across the Space Frontier*, ed. Cornelius Ryan (New York: Viking Press, 1952), 118.

9. Quoted in Ken Wagner, "Salesman on the Moon," *American Mercury* 83 (Aug. 1956): 84.

10. Quoted in "Moon Is on Sale." The article also quotes an anonymous

legal authority's reaction to the moon venture: "I don't know just what's wrong with it. But it's just as illegal as selling the Brooklyn Bridge. A good rule of thumb to follow is: if a man doesn't own it, he can't sell it to you."

11. Wagner, "Salesman on the Moon," 86.

12. See "Robert Coles, Descendent of Town Founders, Dies, Leaves Legacy," *Glen Cove Record Pilot*, Apr. 25, 1985.

13. Peter Ritner, "Who Owns the Moon?" *Saturday Review*, Dec. 7, 1957, 32.

14. Andrew G. Haley, "Can Russia Claim the Moon?" *Washington Post*, Jan. 19, 1958, American Weekly, 2. Also see "Who Will Own the Moon?" *Senior Scholastic*, Mar. 20, 1959, 20–21, which quotes Loftus Becker, a State Department legal adviser, as follows: "The Soviet Union will have to do more than just stick a red flag in the ground to claim territory on the moon." But then there were those such as Pierre Huss who believed that the United States already had a technical claim to the moon. "While possession," he wrote, "is nine-tenths of the law, the landing of men on the Moon . . . is *not* necessary to establish possession." And on what, in Huss's opinion, did the U.S. claim to "technical possession" rest? On January 10, 1946, he pointed out, the U.S. Army Signal Corps made contact with the moon—by radar. See Pierre J. Huss, "Let's Claim the Moon—Now!" *Mechanix Illustrated*, Feb. 1957, 71–72.

15. Wallace E. Howell, Letter to the Editor, *Wall Street Journal*, Sept. 22, 1959, 16, col. 3.

16. Quoted in "Raises Issue of Red Moon Sovereignty," *Chicago Tribune*, Sept 14, 1959, 10, col. 4.

17. Quoted in "Coles Still Claims the Moon Regardless of Russian Rocket," *Glen Cove Record Pilot*, Sept. 17, 1959.

18. When asked if his country was going to lay claim to the satellite, Aleksandr V. Topchiyev of the Soviet Academy of Sciences was emphatic: "No. . . . There will be no territorial claims." (Quoted in "Pleas Are Expected to Mount for U.N. Control of Outer Space," *NYT*, Sept. 15, 1959, 20, col. 6.) It so happened that when the Soviet rocket struck the moon, Nikita Khrushchev was packing his bags for a trip to the United States. Mr. Khrushchev did not arrive in America empty-handed. He brought with him a gift for President Eisenhower, a memento of the historic space shot: a replica of the sphere sent to the moon, complete with Soviet insignia. In a statement, Khrushchev said he expected that when the United States itself launched a mission to the moon, the Soviet pennants would be there to "welcome" the American ones. In a press conference, Eisenhower responded to the Soviet gift. First he joked about the moon ball Khrushchev gave him; then he pointed out that the real one (the full-sized version) with its Soviet pennants was "probably vaporized," putting to rest for the moment any lingering fears about lunar ownership. See the text of Eisenhower's news conference, *NYT*, Sept. 18, 1959, 12, col. 7, question 18.

19. Quoted in "U.S. Rejects Any Flag-Planting as Legal Claim to Rule Moon," *NYT*, Sept. 14, 1959, 1, col. 7.

20. When the U.S. astronauts did land on the moon, they carried with them miniature versions of the flags of 136 nations, plus all 50 states, although only the U.S. flag was actually planted on the moon's surface. See "Of 195 Flags Going to Moon, One Stays," *Business Week*, July 19, 1969, 105.

21. "Who Owns the Moon?" *National Review*, July 15, 1969, 682.

22. I say "few" limits because there were, of course, some more restraining influences at work in America. Consider, for example, the question of territorial sovereignty over Antarctica, which came to a head in the late 1950s as well. Britain, the United States, and the Soviet Union all claimed to have discovered the continent in 1820. Conflicting claims over it continued until a twelve-nation conference in October 1959 proposed a freeze on all territorial claims in the interests of scientific research. The U.S. Senate ratified the Antarctic Pact on August 10, 1960. See Finch, "Territorial Claims," 635–636d.

23. Quoted in Morton J. Horwitz, *The Transformation of American Law, 1870–1960: The Crisis of Legal Orthodoxy* (New York: Oxford Univ. Press, 1992), 145. Also see his discussion of the dephysicalized concept of property, 145–167.

24. Alexander A. Goldenweiser, "Loose Ends of Theory on the Individual, Pattern, and Involution in Primitive Society," in *Essays in Anthropology*, ed. Robert H. Lowie (Berkeley: Univ. of California Press, 1936), 102–103. It was Clifford Geertz who popularized the concept of involution when he applied it to Indonesian agriculture. See Clifford Geertz, *Agricultural Involution: The Processes of Ecological Change in Indonesia* (Berkeley and Los Angeles: Univ. of California Press, 1963).

25. "New Zoning Code Arouses Dispute," *NYT*, May 10, 1959, sec. 8, 1, col. 8.

26. Francis J. Ludes and Harold J. Gilbert, *Corpus Juris Secundum: A Complete Restatement of the Entire American Law as Developed by All Reported Cases* (Brooklyn: American Law Book Co., 1956), 93:594–1078, 94:1–464.

27. Ibid., 93:596.

28. Of course, depending on the location of the resource, it sometimes happens that other systems of rules—such as international law—come into play as well. Consider the mining of deep-sea minerals, which caused a major stir in the 1970s and 1980s. It was then that a number of American companies perfected the technology to profitably mine manganese nodules, potato-shaped lumps containing not just manganese but other valuable minerals such as copper, nickel, and cobalt as well. High concentrations of the nodules were found in an area of the Pacific Ocean stretching west of Mexico to Hawaii. The issue, of course, was who owned the seafloor and the valuable nodules. There were international treaties and laws governing what took place on the surface of the

seas and what could be fished out of them. But until the discovery that the manganese nodules could be mined profitably, no one worried about ownership over the seafloor. In 1967, the Maltese ambassador to the United Nations, Arvid Pardo, proposed that the resources on the seafloor were "the common heritage of mankind." And in 1973, the U.N. convened the Law of the Sea Conference to discuss the matter further and formulate a treaty. The world's developing countries supported the idea of having an international authority that would oversee and regulate deep-sea mining. But the U.S. government, pressed by U.S. companies, opposed the creation of such an international authority because it would place private mining ventures at the mercy of a political entity controlled by poor countries. Then there was the issue of what it meant to say that the seafloor and its resources were "the common heritage of mankind"— language that virtually all nations, including the United States, agreed to in principle. The most common interpretation was that every person, or at least every nation, had part ownership in the deep sea and its resources. But if every nation was part owner of the resource, an international authority, as the developing nations proposed, made good sense. Disturbed by this conclusion, some conservatives in the United States began reconsidering the meaning of the "common heritage" principle. One scholar from the American Enterprise Institute claimed that the phrase really meant that the deep sea was owned by *no one*. And being unowned, the manganese nodules, in this author's opinion, were like any other loose-fish, free for anyone with the money, capital, and know-how—i.e., U.S. companies—to catch and own. As he put it, "Being unowned . . . , the nodules are free for the taking, just as loose fish are in international waters, and no nation or international body has any right to interfere." (Robert A. Goldwin, "Locke and the Law of the Sea," *Commentary* 71 [June 1981]: 48). The Reagan administration eventually refused to sign the international Law of the Sea Treaty and instead, in 1983, proclaimed exclusive rights to the resources in a coastal economic zone that was two hundred miles wide. For the most part, however, U.S. companies have found that mining the deep sea is too costly to make it profitable. Nevertheless, the push to exploit the mineral resources of the oceans continues with new scientific evidence suggesting that volcanic rifts on the ocean floor harbor huge stores of zinc, silver, gold, and copper. See "A Voyage into the Abyss: Gloom, Gold and Godzilla," *NYT*, Nov. 2, 1993, C1. For a discussion of the international and equity issues involved in control over the deep sea, see Richard J. Barnet, *The Lean Years: Politics in the Age of Scarcity* (New York: Simon and Schuster, 1980), 128–131.

29. Henry David Thoreau, *Walden or, Life in the Woods* (1854; reprint, New York: Vintage Books, 1991), 67.

Index